ENGLISH VERB DRILLS

Ed Swick

McGraw Hill

New York   Chicago   San Francisco   Lisbon   London   Madrid   Mexico City
Milan   New Delhi   San Juan   Seoul   Singapore   Sydney   Toronto

1 2 3 4 5 6 7 8 9 10 11 12 13 14 15 16 17 18 19 20 21 22   QPD/QPD   0 9

ISBN 978-0-07-160870-1
MHID   0-07-160870-2
Library of Congress Control Number: 2008935135

McGraw-Hill books are available at special quantity discounts to use as premiums and sales promotions or for use in corporate training programs. To contact a representative, please visit the Contact Us pages at www.mhprofessional.com.

This book is printed on acid-free paper.

Contents

Preface

English Verb Drills is designed to help learners develop the skills that promote effective usage of verbs. It is a vehicle for students of all levels to review and drill conjugational forms, tenses, voice, mood, and verb usage.

Students of language often struggle with the conjugations of verbs. This is particularly true of European languages. One fortunate exception is the English language. Except for the third-person singular conjugation of most verbs, there are no conjugational endings to be considered in the present tense. In the third-person singular, most verbs simply require the ending -s.

Although the conjugation of English verbs is a relatively simple matter, there are other aspects of verbs that require explanation, illustration, and practice. The two most significant of these aspects are *verb irregularities* and *verb usage*. This book identifies the varieties of verb irregularities and provides abundant practice with them. The patterns of verb usage are also explained and illustrated and accompanied by numerous exercises for practice.

At the end of the book is a Mastery Check for learners to verify the development of their skill with all the aspects of verbs provided in the entire book. Besides an Answer Key, there is a useful appendix at the end of the book that provides a complete list of irregular English verbs.

English Verb Drills can serve as an important study aid to all those who wish to perfect their knowledge of English verbs. The book is equally suitable in an English-language classroom or for self-study and is an effective tool for clarifying the complexities and idiosyncrasies of the English verb.

Verbs in the Present and Past Tenses

A tense tells in what time the action of a verb takes place: the present, the past, or the future.

The Present Tense

The base form of a verb is called the infinitive. Infinitives are composed of the particle word **to** and the verb: **to sing, to dance, to develop,** and so on. In the conjugation of a verb in the present tense, the particle word **to** is omitted. The ending **-s** is added to the verb in the third-person singular.

Pronoun	to sleep	to hurry	to belong
I	sleep	hurry	belong
you	sleep	hurry	belong
he / she / it	sleep<u>s</u>	hurr<u>ies</u>	belong<u>s</u>
we	sleep	hurry	belong
they	sleep	hurry	belong

Verbs that end in **-y** change to **-ie-** in the third-person singular conjugation and then add the ending **-s**. However, if the final **-y** of a verb is preceded by a vowel (**a, e, i, o, u**), the **-y** does not change to **-ie-**.

Pronoun	to marry	to try	to fly	to say
I	marry	try	fly	say
you	marry	try	fly	say
he / she / it	marr<u>ies</u>	tr<u>ies</u>	fl<u>ies</u>	say<u>s</u>
we	marry	try	fly	say
they	marry	try	fly	say

For verbs that end in a sound such as **-s, -z, -ch, -tch,** or **-sh,** add the ending **-es** instead of **-s** in the third-person singular conjugation of the present tense.

Pronoun	to miss	to catch	to rush
I	miss	catch	rush
you	miss	catch	rush
he / she / it	misses	catches	rushes
we	miss	catch	rush
they	miss	catch	rush

The ending **-es** is also used as the third-person singular present tense ending for verbs that end in vowels. For example:

I do / he does   I go / he goes

If a verb already ends in **-e**, just add **-s**:

I save / he saves   I believe / he believes

If a noun is used in place of a third-person pronoun, a plural noun will require no ending on the verb, and a singular noun will require the ending **-s**:

the men sing / the man sings   boys run / a boy runs

This conjugational usage with nouns follows the pattern of the plural and singular third-person plural and singular pronouns:

they sing / he, she, it sings   they run / he, she, it runs

Exercise 1

Fill in the blank with the appropriate present tense form of the infinitive provided in parentheses. For example:

John *asks* his father for some advice. (to ask)

1. I never _____ about things I don't understand. (to speak)

2. Mary and I often _____ to the radio in the evening. (to listen)

3. She seldom _____ to keep her room tidy. (to forget)

4. My brother _____ about getting into college. (to worry)

5. The little boy _____ when he doesn't get his way. (to cry)

6. You never _____ my questions directly. (to answer)

7. We _____ Aunt Helen with a beautiful birthday cake. (to surprise)

8. The dog _____ the large bone in the backyard. (to bury)

9. The brothers _____ all their money on video games. (to spend)

10. It usually _____ rather humid in the midafternoon. (to become)

11. They _____ the documents then quickly _____ his office. (to sign / to leave)

12. Bill _____ to borrow my car, but he never _____ me his. (to like / to lend)

13. He _____ the party and _____ for it with his credit card. (to arrange / to pay)

14. I _____ we change the rules and _____ Jim to join our club. (to suggest / to allow)

15. Mark _____ the girl behind the barn and suddenly _____ her. (to catch / to kiss)

To Be and To Have

Two English verbs need to be considered separately because they have a slightly more complicated conjugation in the present tense. These verbs are **to be** and **to have**. The conjugation of these two verbs is significant because, besides being able to function alone in a sentence, they can also serve as auxiliaries of other verbs and in tenses other than the present tense.

Pronoun	to be	to have
I	am	have
you	are	have
he / she / it	is	has
we	are	have
they	are	have

Exercise 2

Fill in the blank with the appropriate present tense form of **to be**.

1. We _____ in the dining room at the table.

2. My sister _____ a rather accomplished pianist.

3. Mark and I _____ both on the soccer team.

4. I _____ interested in learning Arabic.

5. He _____ one of my favorite actors.

6. You _____ my best friend.

7. The women of the village _____ on their way to the capital.

8. It _____ wonderful to see you again.

9. She _____ anxious to go to the dance.

10. They _____ the newest members of our organization.

Fill in the blank with the appropriate present tense form of **to have**.

11. They _____ no time for parties.

12. I rarely _____ enough money.

13. Mr. Roberts _____ an interesting coin collection.

14. He _____ a big surprise for his wife.

15. You _____ a lot of explaining to do.

16. We _____ something to show you.

17. It _____ absolutely no meaning for me.

18. Margaret and I _____ a date to go out for dinner.

19. She _____ my new digital camera.

20. Professor Hill _____ a problem with these lecture dates.

The Past Tense

The English past tense is composed of regular verbs and irregular verbs. Forming the past tense of regular verbs is quite simple: drop the particle word **to** from an infinitive and then add the suffix **-ed**. Verbs that end in **-y** change to **-i-** and then add the ending **-ed**. All persons have the same past tense form.

Pronoun	to look	to marry	to try
I	looked	married	tried
you	looked	married	tried
he / she / it	looked	married	tried
we	looked	married	tried
they	looked	married	tried

However, if the final -y of a verb is preceded by a vowel (a, e, i, o, u), the -y does not change to -i-. In most cases, the suffix -ed is simply added to the verb. Following are a few exceptions:

Pronoun	to play	to pay	to say
I	played	paid	said
you	played	paid	said
he / she / it	played	paid	said
we	played	paid	said
they	played	paid	said

Exercise 3

Fill in the blank of each sentence with the present tense conjugation of the verb provided in parentheses. Then rewrite the sentence in the past tense. For example:

> The children *play* in the garden. (to play)
> *The children played in the garden.*

1. My cousin _____ my lawn mower. (to borrow)

   _____

2. We usually _____ our relatives at holiday time. (to visit)

   _____

3. She _____ for dinner with a personal check. (to pay)

   _____

4. I _____ the boys and girls to some ice cream. (to treat)

   _____

5. He never _____ my instructions. (to follow)

   _____

6. Mr. Jennings _____ a meeting for 5 P.M. (to call)

   _____

7. No one _____ my sister's chocolate cake. (to try)

   _____

8. Rick and Bill _____ that they want to be astronauts. (to say)

   _____

9. They _____ to take a trip to South America. (to plan)

_____

10. It _____ into a complicated problem. (to develop)

_____

Irregular Verbs in the Past Tense

The past tense of irregular verbs is more complex. Some verbs, for example, look identical in both the present and past tenses (with the exception of the third-person singular of the present tense). Some verbs of this type are **to cut, to let, to rid, to bet, to beat, to burst, to fit,** and **to hit.** (See the appendix for a complete list of irregular verbs.) Let's compare the present and past tense of such verbs in the first- and third-person singular.

Infinitive	Present Tense	Past Tense
to cut	I cut / he cuts	I cut / he cut
to hit	I hit / he hits	I hit / he hit
to let	I let / he lets	I let / he let

When just looking at the phrase **you bet,** you cannot tell which tense the verb is in. The context and meaning of the sentence provide the information that tells the tense of the verb. For example:

Yesterday I bet that our team would win. (*"yesterday" = past tense*)
She sets the clock. (*"sets" = conjugated for third-person singular of the present tense*)
They pretend to lose and let me win. (*"pretend" = present tense; therefore,*
   "let" = present tense)

Exercise 4

Using the subject and verb provided, write a sentence in the present tense. Then rewrite the sentence in the past tense. For example:

she / to let
She lets me use her computer.
She let me use her computer.

1. he / to hit

_____

_____

2. it / to burst

_____

_____

3. I / to cut

_____

_____

4. Mark / to fit

_____

_____

5. we / to beat

_____

_____

6. she / to rid

_____

_____

7. Ms. Lopez / to set

_____

_____

8. you / to put

_____

_____

9. they / to wed

_____

_____

10. my brother-in-law / to quit

_____

_____

Irregular Verbs That Change the Base Form

The past tense of many other irregular verbs is created by making a change in the base form of the verb. This usually occurs with a vowel change—for example, **to come → came, to see → saw,**

to know → knew. Let's look at some high-frequency verbs and how they change from the present tense to the past tense.

Infinitive	Present Tense	Past Tense
to speak	I speak / he speaks	I spoke / he spoke
to drive	I drive / he drives	I drove / he drove
to fall	I fall / he falls	I fell / he fell

Not all irregular verbs make only a vowel change in the past tense. Let's look at some that form the past tense by some other irregularity, possibly in addition to a vowel change.

Infinitive	Present Tense	Past Tense
to sell	I sell / he sells	I sold / he sold
to send	I send / he sends	I sent / he sent
to fly	I fly / he flies	I flew / he flew

The verbs **to be** and **to have** in the past tense both have an irregular conjugation. Let's look at the full past tense conjugation of these two important verbs.

Pronoun	to be	to have
I	was	had
you	were	had
he / she / it	was	had
we	were	had
they	were	had

The verb **to go** makes a radical change in the past tense.

Infinitive	Present Tense	Past Tense
to go	I go / he goes	I went / he went

See the appendix for a complete list of verbs that have an irregular past tense formation.

Exercise 5

Write the infinitives provided in the present and past tenses to agree with the pronoun **he.**

1. to show   _____   _____

2. to give   _____   _____

3. to rid   _____   _____

4. to belong   _____   _____

5. to run   _____   _____

6. to make   _____   _____

7. to send   _____   _____

8. to know   _____   _____

9. to tell   _____   _____

10. to explain   _____   _____

11. to wait   _____   _____

12. to please   _____   _____

13. to bring   _____   _____

14. to annoy   _____   _____

15. to pass   _____   _____

16. to win   _____   _____

17. to go   _____   _____

18. to fall   _____   _____

19. to cost   _____   _____

20. to ride   _____   _____

21. to drink   _____   _____

22. to eat   _____   _____

23. to beat   _____   _____

24. to creep   _____   _____

25. to meet   _____   _____

Exercise 6

Rewrite the following present tense sentences in the past tense.

1. Martin speaks with his new professor.

_____

2. I am in a very important meeting.

_____

3. My wife buys a new dress or skirt every month.

_____

4. No one understands his dialect.

_____

5. The lawyers have several contracts to discuss.

_____

6. The poor woman screams in pain.

_____

7. The train leaves at exactly 10 P.M.

_____

8. You are one of the strongest athletes in the school.

_____

9. They build bridges and tunnels.

_____

10. Someone takes them for a drive in the country.

_____

11. Their son grows another inch or two.

_____

12. She has a basket full of colored eggs.

_____

13. We sleep until 9:30 A.M.

_____

14. The butcher weighs the three filets of fish.

_____

15. Mr. Jackson tells another funny story.

_____

Verbs Followed by Infinitives

Perhaps you noticed in some of the example sentences that certain verbs conjugated in the present or the past tense can be followed by another verb in its infinitive form. Some verbs that can be followed by an infinitive are **to attempt, to hope, to forget, to remember, to try,** and **to want.** Compare the similarity of how some of these verbs are used with direct objects and infinitives.

Direct Object: Jack attempted a leap from one cliff to another.
Infinitive: Jack attempted **to leap** from one cliff to another.

Direct Object: She forgets her keys and purse.
Infinitive: She forgets **to take** her keys and purse.

Direct Object: I remember the last time I saw her.
Infinitive: I remember **to send** her a birthday card.

Direct Object: He tries some tapioca pudding.
Infinitive: He tries **to swallow** some tapioca pudding.

Direct Object: Nobody wants cold pizza.
Infinitive: Nobody wants **to eat** cold pizza.

Exercise 7

Rewrite each sentence, changing the direct object to any appropriate infinitive phrase. For example:

She attempted a difficult move.
She attempted to do a backflip.

1. Bill wanted a piece of pizza.

   _____

2. No one remembers her birthday.

   _____

3. I tried a spoonful of the soup.

   _____

4. Uncle James forgot his wallet again.

   _____

5. Tina attempts a dangerous trick.

   _____

2

Auxiliaries of Tense

In the present and past tenses, verbs are conjugated in a way that infers a present action (**he speaks**) or a past action (**he spoke**). But in the other tenses, auxiliaries are conjugated and verbs appear as infinitives or past participles. Infinitives are the base form of a verb and are often preceded by the particle word **to** (**to go** or **go**, **to be** or **be**). Regular past participles end in -ed (**have looked**, **have talked**) and irregular past participles take a variety of different forms (**have seen**, **have met**, **have spoken**, and so on). The three auxiliaries that help to form the other tenses are **will**, **shall**, and **have**.

Will and *Shall*

Will

The verb **to will** has a limited use as a transitive verb. It means that someone exercises his desire to do something or to use his own will. It can be used in various tenses but tends to be used in modern English in the present and past.

> God wills it, and therefore it must be done.
> The sickly man willed himself well.

But this verb's primary use in modern English is as one of the auxiliaries of the future tense. It is followed by an infinitive (with the particle word **to** omitted). It has the same form with all persons.

I will speak	we will learn
you will understand	you will help
he / she / it will answer	they will travel

Shall

The verb **shall** is the other auxiliary of the future tense. It is followed by an infinitive (with the particle word **to** omitted). It has the same form with all persons.

I shall write	we shall overcome
you shall study	you shall remain silent
he / she / it shall begin	they shall stand

There is a difference between **will** and **shall**: traditionally, **shall** is used with the first-person singular and plural, and **will** is used with the second- and third-persons singular and plural.

I shall speak	we shall learn
you will understand	you will help
he / she / it will answer	they will travel

However, when the future tense infers a promise, threat, or command or is intended for emphasis, the two verbs are used in just the opposite manner.

I will speak	we will learn
you shall understand	you shall help
he / she / it shall answer	they shall travel

Remember that a noun or pronoun combined with **and I** can be replaced by the pronoun **we**: **Mr. Smith and I = we / she and I = we**. This will affect your choice of **will** or **shall**.

This is important: over time, the contemporary tendency has been to use **will** in place of **shall** with all persons in the future tense.

Exercise 8

Rewrite the following sentences in the "traditional" future tense. Then rewrite them as a "promise."

1. He plays the piano.

_____

_____

2. I study English.

_____

_____

3. We buy a new house.

_____

_____

4. She loves the book.

_____

_____

5. Mark makes no mistakes.

_____

_____

6. The boys help them.

_____

_____

7. No one is there.

_____

_____

8. You eat enough.

_____

_____

9. It needs work.

_____

_____

10. They practice daily.

_____

_____

11. Tina receives the money.

_____

_____

12. I repair the radio.

_____

_____

13. The woman kisses him.

_____

_____

14. We drive slowly.

_____

_____

15. You stand up.

_____

_____

16. She says nothing.

_____

_____

17. Everyone gives ten dollars.

_____

_____

18. Bill and I spend less money.

_____

_____

19. It breaks down.

_____

_____

20. He pretends.

_____

_____

Exercise 9

Rewrite the following past tense phrases in the "contemporary" future tense.

1. she ate _____

2. I looked _____

3. no one understood _____

4. Mr. Wills found _____

5. we spoke _____

6. Jim and I went _____

7. she heard _____

8. they jumped _____

9. Ms. Garcia cut _____

10. you were _____

11. the men drank _____

12. it seemed _____

13. something happened _____

14. nothing stopped _____

15. he saw _____

16. you bought _____

17. I thought _____

18. we hurried _____

19. the child cried _____

20. it had _____

When the future tense is expressed as a question, the auxiliary is the first element of the future tense sentence, and, in most cases, the "traditional" use of **will** and **shall** must be used. For example:

First-Person Singular	Shall I help?	Shall I leave?
Second-Person Singular	Will you help?	Will you leave?
Third-Person Singular	Will he help?	Will he leave?
	Will she help?	Will she leave?
	Will it help?	Will it leave?
First-Person Plural	Shall we help?	Shall we leave?
Second-Person Plural	Will you help?	Will you leave?
Third-Person Plural	Will they help?	Will they leave?

If **will** and **shall** are not used in this way in questions, the questions sound awkward: "Will I help?" is awkward; "Shall you leave?" is also awkward.

Exercise 10

Rewrite the following present and past tense sentences as future tense questions.

1. He spends a lot of money. _____
2. They hurried home. _____
3. I buy this blouse. _____
4. Donald studied here. _____
5. Bill was in Europe. _____
6. We helped them. _____
7. My cousins live in New York. _____
8. You lost your wallet again. _____
9. She fell down. _____
10. It smells good. _____
11. The boys and I play checkers. _____
12. You spell it correctly. _____
13. A woman becomes president. _____
14. Someone forgot this book. _____
15. I am your partner. _____
16. You and I work together. _____
17. My answer was right. _____
18. They swam to shore. _____
19. Her questions were difficult. _____
20. We played in a band. _____
21. Sarah became a doctor. _____
22. He sang in the choir. _____
23. The plant grew fast. _____
24. Someone helps me. _____
25. That hurts. _____

Have

When **to have** is used as a transitive verb, its conjugation is as follows:

I have	we have
you have	you have
he / she / it has	they have

Because **to have** is a transitive verb, it can be followed by a direct object.

I have a <u>story</u> to tell you.
She has a <u>problem</u> with her computer.

But when a conjugation of **to have** is followed by a past participle, it forms one of the perfect tenses: the present perfect tense, the past perfect tense, or the future perfect tense. Regular past participles look like the past tense; they have the ending -ed: **jumped, cried, looked,** and so on. Irregular participles are formed in different ways. Following are some examples with high-frequency verbs:

Infinitive	Have + Irregular Past Participle
to bring	have brought
to cut	have cut
to go	have gone
to see	have seen
to send	have sent
to speak	have spoken
to take	have taken
to write	have written

See the appendix for a list of all irregular past participles.

The Present Perfect Tense

When the auxiliary **have** is conjugated in the present tense and is followed by a regular or an irregular past participle, the tense is called the present perfect tense. It is only the third-person singular where the auxiliary **have** changes to **has.**

I have learned   we have understood
you have taken   you have noticed
he has been   they have found
she has drunk
it has fallen

Use the present perfect tense to say that an action began in the past and has continued until the present. For example:

He has spoken English for two years. (*He began to speak English two years ago. He still speaks English.*)

Exercise 11

Rewrite each of the following phrases in the present perfect tense.

1. I find _____

2. they begin _____

3. Mark thinks _____

4. she studies _____

5. we arrange _____

6. it breaks _____

7. you pretend _____

8. he is _____

9. Ms. Brown forgets _____

10. each boy tries _____

11. Tom and I dance _____

12. the woman knit _____

13. someone shouts _____

14. I know _____

15. you come _____

16. it rains _____

17. no one remembers _____

18. we lend _____

19. someone knocks _____

20. it bleeds _____

21. you have _____

22. they are _____

23. Maria allows _____

24. we spend _____

25. it costs _____

The Past Perfect Tense

The past perfect tense consists of the past tense of **have** followed by a regular or an irregular participle.

I had said   we had borrowed

you had broken   you had written

he had changed   they had been

she had had

it had started

This tense is used when an action began in the past and also ended in the past. For example:

He had spoken English for two years. (*Ten years ago he began to speak English. Eight years ago he stopped speaking English.*)

Exercise 12

Rewrite the following present and past tense phrases in the past perfect tense.

1. we became _____

2. I cried _____

3. you follow _____

4. someone hit _____

5. they called _____

6. the boys play _____

7. she sings _____

8. it rang _____

9. the clouds move _____

10. I drive _____

11. the girls and I laugh _____

12. it stormed _____

13. he marries _____

14. John weds _____

15. we fly _____

The Future Perfect Tense

The future perfect tense consists of **will** or **shall** followed by **have** and a regular or an irregular past participle.

> I will (shall) have spoken   we will (shall) have made
> you will have been   you will have had
> he will have noticed   they will have stolen
> she will have phoned
> it will have happened

This tense is used when an action began in the past and will end in the future. For example:

> He will have graduated by June. (*He began his studies in the past. In the future month of June he will graduate.*)

Use the "contemporary" or "traditional" rules for **will** and **shall** with the perfect tenses.

Exercise 13

Rewrite the following present and past tense phrases in the future perfect tense.

1. my landlady said _____

2. you bargain _____

3. they travel _____

4. she spends _____

5. someone reminded _____

6. it was _____

7. Martin has _____

8. I belong _____

9. we sold _____

10. life is _____

11. my daughter became _____

12. it ends _____

13. they died _____

14. an explorer climbs _____

15. he knew _____

Adding Infinitive Phrases

Just as infinitives and infinitive phrases can follow certain verbs in the present and past tenses, the same verbs in the perfect and future tenses can be followed by infinitives and infinitive phrases as well. Some of these verbs are:

hope	forget
try	attempt
remember	manage
seem	arrange
want	agree
appear	promise
pretend	learn
prepare	refuse
fail	learn

In the perfect and future tenses, such verbs follow the pattern of this example:

Present Perfect: I have forgotten to lock the door.
Past Perfect: I had forgotten to lock the door.
Future Perfect: I will have forgotten to lock the door.
Future: I will forget to lock the door.

Exercise 14

Complete each sentence with any appropriate infinitive phrase. For example:

She had hoped to *climb to the top of the mountain*.

1. Somebody will remember to _____.
2. We have forgotten to _____.
3. I have tried to _____.
4. Somebody has attempted to _____.
5. Will he manage to _____?
6. The weather had seemed to _____.
7. She will arrange to _____.
8. I had wanted to _____.
9. The lawyers have agreed to _____.
10. You have failed to _____.
11. We have promised to _____.
12. The boys will have learned to _____.
13. The women will ask to _____.
14. Several of them had prepared to _____.
15. I will have failed to _____.

3

Linking and Intransitive Verbs

Linking Verbs

To Be

Linking verbs combine the subject of a sentence with an adjective, a noun, or a pronoun that follows the verb. This occurs most frequently with the verb **to be**.

I am cold	we are happy
you are alone	you are my friend
he is talented	they are sad
she is a lawyer	
it is you	

The same structure remains as the verb changes tenses.

Present: he is glad
Past: he was glad
Present Perfect: he has been glad
Past Perfect: he had been glad
Future Perfect: he will have been glad
Future: he will be glad

In informal style, it is common to use an objective case pronoun after **to be**. In formal style, subjective case pronouns are used.

Subjective Case	**Objective Case**
It is I.	It is me.

Exercise 15

Complete each sentence with any appropriate adjective.

1. Ms. Thomas is _____.
2. I am very _____.
3. You will be _____.
4. Someone was _____ about your answer.
5. It has been quite _____.
6. We will always be _____.
7. She has never been _____ with this apartment.

Complete the following sentences with any appropriate noun phrase.

8. My boss was _____ of the committee.
9. Tom and I have been _____ for many years.
10. She will be _____.
11. I always wanted to be _____.
12. We are _____.
13. They were _____.

Complete the following sentences with any appropriate pronoun.

14. Bill is not _____.
15. It was _____.

Other Linking Verbs

Other linking verbs work in the same manner as **to be**: they combine the subject of a sentence with an adjective that follows the verb. Some of these linking verbs can also be combined with nouns and pronouns that follow the verb. The verbs that are followed only by adjectives are:

appear	seem
feel	smell
grow	sound
look	stay
prove	taste

Each of these ten verbs can be followed by an adjective that modifies the subject of the sentence, and this can occur in any tense and with auxiliaries.

> The man **appears** ill.
> She **feels** unhappy.
> The sky **has grown** dark.
> His skin **will look** better tomorrow.
> Their theory **proves** wrong.
> The man **seemed** impatient.
> Her cookies **have** always **smelled** so good.
> The piano **will sound** better after tuning.
> She wants **to stay** young.
> The soup **tasted** delicious.

Exercise 16

Complete each of the following sentences with any appropriate adjective.

1. The flowers smell so _____.

2. No one can stay _____ forever.

3. One of the men appeared very _____.

4. I have always felt _____ when visiting you.

5. The moon grows _____ as the clouds come in.

6. This salad tastes _____.

7. Their rock band never sounded _____.

8. His answer proved _____.

9. Their new car looked _____.

10. Mr. Phillips always seems so _____.

Two linking verbs (**to become** and **to remain**) can be followed by adjectives, nouns, and on rare occasions pronouns and can be used in any tense and with auxiliaries. For example:

> The weather became awful. (*adjective*)
> Betty wants to become a lawyer. (*noun*)

> The lake remained calm. (*adjective*)
> Bill hoped to remain an architect. (*noun*)

The verb **to seem** can sometimes be followed by a modified noun.

That seems a strange statement to me.

Exercise 17

Complete the following sentences twice: once with an adjective or adjective phrase and once with a noun or noun phrase.

1. This will become _____ for them.

   This will become _____ for them.

2. Mary became _____.

   Mary became _____.

3. My father wanted to remain _____.

   My father wanted to remain _____.

4. She remained _____.

   She remained _____.

Linking Verbs as Transitive Verbs

Some of the linking verbs can also be used as transitive verbs. That is, they do not combine a subject with an adjective that follows them, but, instead, they take a direct object. Compare the following sentences. Each direct object is underlined.

Linking Verb	Transitive Verb
She feels happy.	She feels the fabric.
The cake smelled burned.	Bill smelled the flowers.
It grows dark.	They grow tropical plants.
The music sounds loud.	He sounds the alarm.
It proved wrong.	She proved the theory.
The soup tastes salty.	Mom tastes the soup.

It is easy to determine whether these verbs are used as linking verbs or as transitive verbs. Replace the verb with an appropriate form of **to be**. If the sentence still makes sense, the verb is a linking verb. If it makes no sense, the verb is a transitive verb. For example:

Jim felt very lonely. → Jim *was* very lonely. (*makes sense = linking verb*)

Jim felt a pain in his arm. → Jim *was* a pain in his arm. (*makes no sense = transitive verb*)

The jam will taste sweet. → The jam *will be* sweet. (*makes sense = linking verb*)

I will taste the jam. → I *will be* the jam. (*makes no sense = transitive verb*)

Exercise 18

In the blank provided, write the letter *L* if the verb in the sentence is a linking verb. Write the letter *T* if the verb in the sentence is a transitive verb.

_____ 1. Someone has been very naughty.

_____ 2. My sister wants to become a doctor.

_____ 3. I immediately smelled her perfume.

_____ 4. This bed has never felt uncomfortable before.

_____ 5. Grandmother remained very angry at us.

_____ 6. She has been a teacher for many years.

_____ 7. We need to sound the fire alarm.

_____ 8. My glass of milk tastes sour.

_____ 9. I can smell the smoke from their campfire.

_____ 10. In June it usually becomes rainy.

_____ 11. The cellar always appeared dirty.

_____ 12. You seem rather nervous.

_____ 13. My aunt remained a pilot until she was sixty.

_____ 14. The necklace proved worthless.

_____ 15. You will never be a successful actor.

_____ 16. They grow only wheat and corn here.

_____ 17. Those puppies looked so unhealthy.

_____ 18. The guards will stay alert.

_____ 19. It was you!

_____ 20. The tone of her voice sounds lovely.

Intransitive Verbs

Transitive verbs can take a direct or an indirect object. Intransitive verbs *cannot*. They can be followed by adverbs and prepositional phrases, but they can never take an object. The objects in the following sentences are underlined.

<table>
<tr><td>Verbs with an Object</td><td>Verbs Having No Object</td></tr>
<tr><td>Bill borrowed <u>his father's car</u>.</td><td>Bill ran into the street.</td></tr>
<tr><td>I lost <u>my new gloves</u>.</td><td>I fell over Bobby's wagon.</td></tr>
<tr><td>She signed <u>all the documents</u>.</td><td>She flew from New York to London.</td></tr>
</table>

However, some verbs can act as either a transitive or an intransitive verb. Let's look at some verbs that can be either transitive or intransitive.

<table>
<tr><td>Transitive Verb</td><td>Intransitive Verb</td></tr>
<tr><td>He ran <u>the new machinery</u>.</td><td>He ran around the track.</td></tr>
<tr><td>She flew <u>her own plane</u>.</td><td>She flew there on a plane.</td></tr>
<tr><td>I want to drive <u>your new car</u>.</td><td>I want to drive to Denver.</td></tr>
</table>

A few verbs come in pairs: one verb in the pair is transitive, and the other verb is intransitive. The verbs are shown in **bold**.

<table>
<tr><td>Transitive Verb</td><td>Intransitive Verb</td></tr>
<tr><td>Carmen lays the books on the table.</td><td>The books lie next to the computer.</td></tr>
<tr><td>We set the vase on the piano.</td><td>The little boy sits under the table.</td></tr>
</table>

In all cases, when you are determining whether a verb is transitive or intransitive, it is the use of an object with the verb that is the clue that it is transitive. Let's look at some sentences that illustrate intransitive verbs. Note the regular use of adverbs and prepositional phrases in these sentences.

The man **died** after a long illness.
The guests **will arrive** at 8 P.M.
My sister **has come** home for the holidays.
They excitedly **hurried** up the steps.
Someday we **will journey** to Mars.
The woman **had swum** across the English Channel.
Tom always **sleeps** so late.

Exercise 19

In the blank provided, write the letter *T* if the sentence has a transitive verb. Write the letter *I* if the sentence has an intransitive verb.

_____ 1. We always take the train into the city.

_____ 2. Someone slapped me on the back.

_____ 3. It rains every evening.

_____ 4. Jake stopped the car in front of a store.

_____ 5. A stranger came up to the door.

_____ 6. I sit next to her bed.

_____ 7. The boys broke the window.

_____ 8. Tina wants to travel to Asia.

_____ 9. He thought about his girlfriend back home.

_____ 10. They will drive to Los Angeles.

_____ 11. Mark sped down the highway.

_____ 12. You know nothing about my problems.

_____ 13. Tim and I had never run so fast before.

_____ 14. The artist painted my portrait.

_____ 15. All the plants died from the cold.

_____ 16. Professor Wilde shook my hand slowly.

_____ 17. I touched her warm skin.

_____ 18. The little boy suddenly fell from his chair.

_____ 19. They went home.

_____ 20. It snowed during the night.

_____ 21. Somehow Marie got another cold.

_____ 22. A parade of ants crept across the kitchen floor.

_____ 23. Dad looks out the window.

_____ 24. The children want a puppy.

_____ 25. Bobby wants to go to the circus.

4

Modal Auxiliaries

A modal auxiliary tells the mode or manner in which an action is performed. The mode or manner suggests a degree of obligation, enjoyment, or desire to carry out the action. Modal auxiliaries fall into two categories: (1) those that are followed by an infinitive that includes the particle word **to** and (2) those that omit the particle word **to**. For example:

I have **to go** home.   I must **go** home.

Modals and Infinitives with *To*

The following list of modal auxiliaries contains those that are followed by an infinitive with **to**. The meaning provided shows the degree of obligation, enjoyment, or desire to carry out the action of an accompanying infinitive.

Modal Auxiliary	Meaning
be able to	have the ability
be allowed to	have permission
be supposed to	moderate obligation
be to	moderate obligation
have got to	emphasized strong obligation
have to	strong obligation
like to	enjoy an action
need to	necessary obligation
ought to	moderate obligation
used to	regular action in the past
want to	desire
wish to	desire

The modals that are part of a phrase that begins with **be** conjugate only the verb **be**.

Pronoun	be allowed to	be supposed to	be to
I	am allowed to	am supposed to	am to
you	are allowed to	are supposed to	are to
he / she / it	is allowed to	is supposed to	is to
we	are allowed to	are supposed to	are to
they	are allowed to	are supposed to	are to

The other modals conjugate the initial verb in the phrase. Here are some examples:

Pronoun	have to	need to	want to
I	have to	need to	want to
you	have to	need to	want to
he / she / it	has to	needs to	wants to
we	have to	need to	want to
they	have to	need to	want to

A *word of caution:* do not confuse the three uses of **to have:**

Transitive Verb: He **has** a new job. (**have** *followed by a direct object*)
Perfect Tense Auxiliary: We **have** arrived. (**have** *followed by past participle*)
Modal Auxiliary: We **have to** stay home. (**have** *followed by infinitive*)

Various modals can be used with the same infinitive phrase. The modal changes the mode or manner of the action of the accompanying infinitive—not its meaning.

I am allowed to play the piano.
I am supposed to play the piano.
I have to play the piano.
I wish to play the piano.

Exercise 20

Combine the modal auxiliaries provided with the phrases in parentheses. Keep the same subject in the phrase in parentheses. For example:

I go home for supper. (be to / want to)
I am to go home for supper.
I want to go home for supper.

1. She stays with her mother. (be supposed to / need to / wish to)

_____

_____

_____

2. They perform in a circus. (want to / used to / have got to)

_____

_____

_____

3. You memorize the poem. (have to / be to / ought to)

_____

_____

_____

4. We relax in the garden. (like to / be allowed to / need to)

_____

_____

_____

5. Jim is a good cook. (wish to / want to / be supposed to)

_____

_____

_____

Tenses

Most modal auxiliaries can occur in other tenses. Look at the following examples given with the pronoun **he**.

Tense	be allowed to	have to	need to
Present	he is allowed to	he has to	he needs to
Past	he was allowed to	he had to	he needed to
Present Perfect	he has been allowed to	he has had to	he has needed to
Past Perfect	he had been allowed to	he had had to	he had needed to
Future	he will be allowed to	he will have to	he will need to

Some of the modal auxiliaries cannot be formed in all the tenses. **Ought to** and **be to** should only be used in the present and past tenses. These modals sound awkward in other tenses.

> **Present:** You ought to stay home tonight.
> **Past:** You ought to have stayed home tonight.

> **Present:** She is to hurry home.
> **Past:** She was to hurry home.

Notice in the past tense meaning that **ought to** is followed by **have** and a past participle. This occurs with any accompanying phrase that begins with **have** and a past participle.

> She ought to have spent less money.
> We ought to have gone home earlier.

The modal **used to** always infers an action that has taken place regularly in the past. It cannot be used in other tenses.

> I used to live in Australia.
> My cousin used to work in that factory.
> There used to be a drugstore on that corner.

A word of caution: you must distinguish the use of **used to** from two similar verbs: **be used to** and **used to be**. **Be used to** is a synonym for *be accustomed to*. **Used to be** is a synonym for *formerly was / were*. Let's look at some examples.

> I **used to speak** German. (*modal auxiliary showing a regular action in the past*)
> I **am used to** life in America. ("*I am accustomed to life in America.*")
> I **used to be** a fireman. ("*I was formerly a fireman.*")

The modal **have got to** sounds awkward in other tenses. Use it in the present tense to emphasize the obligation inferred by **have to**.

Normal Obligation	**Emphatic Obligation**
You have to help me.	You have got to help me.
I have to rush home.	I have got to rush home.

Exercise 21

Rewrite the following phrases in the tenses provided. If a modal cannot be written in a given tense, place an *X* in that blank.

1. I am supposed to play.

Past _____

Present Perfect _____

Future _____

2. She wants to learn.

Past _____

Present Perfect _____

Future _____

3. They ought to hurry.

Past _____

Present Perfect _____

Future _____

4. No one likes to eat it.

Past _____

Present Perfect _____

Future _____

5. We are allowed to listen.

Past _____

Present Perfect _____

Future _____

6. Betty needs to rest.

Past _____

Present Perfect _____

Future _____

7. Someone has to help.

Past _____

Present Perfect _____

Future _____

8. Mr. Lee used to work here.

Past _____

Present Perfect _____

Future _____

9. You are to help them.

Past _____

Present Perfect _____

Future _____

10. Someone has got to listen.

Past _____

Present Perfect _____

Future _____

Modals with Infinitives That Omit *To*

The modal auxiliaries that omit the particle word **to** from an infinitive are listed here:

> can
> could
> had better (better)
> may
> might
> must
> should
> would

They combine with infinitives in the same way that **will** and **shall** do.

He **will go** home.   We **shall speak** with her.

The modals of this type do not have conjugational endings. They are identical in all the persons.

Pronoun	can	might	should
I	can	might	should
you	can	might	should
he / she / it	can	might	should
we	can	might	should
they	can	might	should

Tenses

These modals tend to be used in the present tense, but many of them have a subjunctive mood meaning. That is, they express what might be a possibility or a probability in the future or if a certain condition is met. And they are in reality the past tense of other auxiliaries.

Present	Past
can	could
may	might
shall	should
will	would

In sentences they are used like this:

I can understand you. (*present tense*)

I could understand you. (*past tense*)

I could understand you if you spoke louder. (*subjunctive "if you spoke louder" = a condition*)

That may be true. (*present tense*)

That might be true. (*past tense*)

He might return if you called him. (*subjunctive "if you called him" = a condition*)

We shall hurry there. (*future tense*)

We should hurry there. (*subjunctive = the probable thing to do*)

No one will know. (*future tense*)

No one would know. (*subjunctive = the probable outcome*)

Must and **had better** (often said as **better**) are used only in the present tense.

You must help me.   You had better help me. (You better help me.)

A *word of caution:* do not confuse the normal use of the modal **must** (strong obligation) with its idiomatic form **must be** + **present participle**. Compare the following pairs of sentences:

I must remain at home tonight. (*I have to remain at home tonight.*)
I must **be dreaming**. (*I feel that this is a dream and not real.*)

You must pay your bill. (*You have to pay your bill.*)
You must **be joking**. (*I feel you are not serious. This is a joke.*)

Most of the modal auxiliaries of this type can be combined with **have** plus a past participle. When this occurs, the meaning suggests a past action with a wished for or preferred outcome. Consider these example sentences:

You could have told me that earlier. (*You had the ability to tell me, but you did not.*)
She had better have found the money. (*a warning that this is the desired outcome*)
I may have forgotten about it. (*It is possible that I forgot.*)
Your wallet might have been stolen. (*It is possible the wallet is not lost but was stolen.*)
They must have lost their way. (*It is likely that they are lost.*)
We should have phoned first. (*It was wrong not to phone first.*)
Ben would have helped you. (*You were sure to have received Ben's help.*)

Exercise 22

Rewrite the sentences provided with the modal auxiliaries in parentheses.

1. The team hurries to the stadium. (must)

_____

2. Someone unlocks the door for you. (can)

_____

3. Tim studies hard for his final exams. (had better)

_____

4. I learn as much as I can about her. (would)

_____

5. This is a good way to get to know one another. (may)

_____

6. Charles comes along when we visit Graceland. (might)

_____

7. Everyone uses good manners. (should)

_____

8. Erik speaks with his angry neighbors. (could have)

_____

9. Your son has the money for the payment. (had better have)

_____

10. Perhaps she needs some help. (may have)

_____

11. Someone sees the accident happen. (might have)

_____

12. They go to the movies. (must have)

_____

13. You get more sleep. (should have)

_____

14. I plan a party for you. (would have)

_____

15. My friends vote in the election. (better)

_____

Exercise 23

Rewrite the sentences provided with the modal auxiliaries in parentheses. The modals provided here represent various types and tenses.

1. The students report to the auditorium. (be to)

_____

2. My parents spend a lot of time in the country. (have to)

_____

3. Mark asks a better question. (ought to have)

_____

4. The boys fall asleep. (must have)

_____

5. This is the right thing to do. (might)

_____

6. They see a house in the distance. (could)

_____

7. No one touches his stamp collection. (be allowed to)

_____

8. This is a good lesson for you. (should)

_____

9. I listen to my father. (should have)

_____

10. Mr. Bennett speaks three languages. (can)

_____

11. She forgets my name. (may have)

_____

12. The girls leave the meeting early. (had to)

_____

13. I sometimes nap after work. (have needed to)

_____

14. They hold down their voices. (ought to)

_____

15. Dad plays games with the children. (like to)

_____

16. The Johnsons live across the street from us. (used to)

_____

17. I see the anger in his eyes. (could)

_____

18. He washes the dishes every day. (was supposed to)

_____

19. Maria returns to Miami. (will have to)

_____

20. We always travel to Korea. (have wanted to)

_____

21. The hikers take the path on the right. (were to)

_____

22. You have a good excuse. (had better)

_____

23. She becomes a ballerina. (wished to)

_____

24. The neighbors upstairs stop the noise. (have got to)

_____

25. My brother takes the bus to work. (will have to)

_____

5

Complete and Incomplete Actions

Complete Actions

English uses verbs in a way that shows the difference between an action that is complete and an action that is incomplete. So far, you have seen verbs in the form that shows an action that is complete. The same verbs can also suggest that the action is a habit. In the present tense, it is not always clear whether an action is complete, but the suggestion of a habit is obvious.

Present Tense

> We tour the art museum. (*This is not a habit. It is an action that is presumed complete in the present time.*)
> Jack sings in the choir. (*His habit is to sing in the choir.*)
> I borrow money from Jake. (*This may or may not be a habit. It may be an action that is presumed complete in the present time.*)
> My uncle collects stamps. (*The uncle's habit is to collect stamps.*)

Often adverbs tell that an action is done regularly or as a habit. The use of such adverbs makes clear with what regularity the action of the verb is performed.

> I <u>always</u> arrive to work on time.
> We <u>sometimes</u> picnic on the beach.
> Bill <u>rarely</u> finishes a project.

Other adverbs that indicate that an action is done regularly or as a habit include the following:

all the time	most of the time
constantly	never
continually	occasionally
every (day, week, etc.)	often

five times a year	once a day
four times a month	persistently
frequently	regularly
habitually	seldom
half of the time	twice a week
hardly ever	usually

When the verb **have** is conjugated as a transitive verb, it shows an action that is complete or done regularly or as a habit, especially when accompanied by an appropriate adverb. For example:

I have a special gift for you. I <u>always</u> have a special gift for you.

Mark has the jitters before a concert. <u>Most of the time</u>, Mark has the jitters before a concert.

My aunt has tea with me. My aunt has tea with me <u>every day</u>.

Linking verbs can also suggest that an action is complete in the present time or is a habit or done regularly if accompanied by an appropriate adverb.

My sister seems quite happy. My sister <u>always</u> seems quite happy.

He becomes bored with this game. He <u>often</u> becomes bored with this game.

This mattress feels more comfortable. This mattress <u>usually</u> feels more comfortable.

I am shocked. I am <u>never</u> shocked.

Past Tense

It is easier to differentiate between a completed action and a regular or habitual action in the past tense, because that action has already been performed.

He returned to the library. (*Complete. He arrived at the library.*)

He sometimes returned to the library by noon. (*His occasional habit was to return to the library by noon.*)

I bought a new car. (*Complete. I already own the new car.*)

I rarely bought a car from that dealer. (*It was not often that I bought a car from that dealer.*)

June built a birdhouse. (*Complete. The birdhouse is finished and ready for birds.*)

June built a birdhouse every spring. (*June's habit was to build a birdhouse every spring.*)

Exercise 24

Rewrite each past tense sentence with any appropriate adverb.

1. Mr. Kelly fixed the old car.

_____

2. I borrowed ten dollars from her.

_____

3. We were interested in his poems.

_____

4. My grandfather had a serious illness.

_____

5. Each day became longer and longer.

_____

6. It smelled awful in his room.

_____

7. John went to school with his little sister.

_____

8. The twins liked turkey sandwiches.

_____

9. My uncle made a large salad for supper.

_____

10. They traveled to Asia.

_____

11. I spent my last dollar.

_____

12. Andrea danced with the young man from France.

_____

13. We began the lesson from Chapter 2.

_____

14. The girls were late to soccer practice.

_____

15. You spoke in German with her.

_____

16. The sheets felt damp.

_____

17. Everyone had a good time at my party.

_____

18. My neighbor came by for a visit.

_____

19. Barbara took the children for a walk.

_____

20. Tim and I lived off the land.

_____

The Perfect Tenses

Verbs in the present and past perfect tenses indicate a completed action, and with appropriate adverbs they show a regular or habitual action. These two tenses consist of the verb **have** or **had**, respectively, and are accompanied by a past participle.

> I have seen that movie. (*complete*)
> I have seen that movie several times. (*habitual action*)

> We have spoken with Jack. (*complete*)
> We have occasionally spoken with Jack. (*habitual action*)

> My wife had baked a cake. (*complete*)
> My wife had often baked a cake for my birthday. (*habitual action*)

> He had borrowed money from me. (*complete*)
> He had rarely borrowed money from me. (*habitual action*)

The verb **to be** and linking verbs show completed and habitual actions in the same way in these tenses.

> She has been in Mexico. She has never been in Mexico.
> I had been her best friend. I had always been her best friend.

He has seemed very angry. He has sometimes seemed very angry.
He had appeared arrogant. He had usually appeared arrogant.

Future Tense

The idea of a completed action or one of regularity or habit is also apparent in the future tense.

Jane will sing a song for us. Jane will often sing a song for us.
I will buy some groceries there. I will occasionally buy some groceries there.
We will have a party on the weekend. We will sometimes have a party on the weekend.

This also occurs with **to be** and linking verbs.

I will be bored with the project. I will never be bored with the project.
His ideas will prove wrong. His ideas will always prove wrong.

Exercise 25

Read each past tense sentence. Write the letter *C* in the blank provided if the action of the verb is complete. Or write the letter *H* in the blank provided if the action of the verb is regular or habitual. Then rewrite the sentences in the present perfect and future tenses. For example:

H She often studied at home.
She has often studied at home.
She will often study at home.

_____ 1. My cousin broke the vase.

_____

_____

_____ 2. We never played chess.

_____

_____

_____ 3. I usually wrote my letters in pencil.

_____

_____

_____ 4. There was a loud noise in the hall.

_____

_____

_____ 5. Someone knocked at the door.

_____

_____

_____ 6. Laura wanted a diamond ring.

_____

_____

_____ 7. Most of the time, she worked in a drugstore.

_____

_____

_____ 8. My son visited me once a year.

_____

_____

_____ 9. The men frequently stopped for a cool drink.

_____

_____

_____ 10. I continually asked for your help.

_____

_____

_____ 11. She rarely risked her money on a bet.

_____

_____

_____ 12. Donald fainted.

_____

_____

_____ 13. We watered the lawn every day.

_____

_____

_____ 14. The boys hardly ever helped us.

_____

_____

_____ 15. I was in Chicago for a week.

_____

_____

Incomplete Actions

An incomplete action can be shown by using a form of the verb **to be** followed by a present participle. Present participles are formed by adding the suffix **-ing** to an infinitive.

go → going   hurry → hurrying   come → coming

When used in sentences, this kind of structure says that the action of the verb is still in progress or incomplete. For example:

I **am going** to the bus stop. (*I'm on my way. I have not arrived there yet.*)
She **is speaking** on the phone. (*Her phone conversation is not yet complete.*)
The men **are working** hard. (*The work is in progress and not yet complete.*)

This usage of **to be** and a present participle can occur in all the tenses.

Present
We are driving to California.
She is sleeping.

Past
Someone was looking in the window.
You were sitting at the computer.

Present and Past Perfect
Tom has been working here for two years.
I had been waiting for a long time.

Future and Future Perfect

The girls will be taking ballet lessons.

I will have been working for him for eight years by this time next week.

Exercise 26

In the blank provided, write the letter *C* if the action of the verb is complete or habitual. Write the letter *I* if the action of the verb is incomplete or in progress.

_____ 1. She has been studying for the bar exam.

_____ 2. No one saw the accident take place.

_____ 3. We usually sit in the balcony.

_____ 4. Dad has been working at the same job for years.

_____ 5. I am baking an apple pie.

_____ 6. Daniel suddenly rushed into the living room.

_____ 7. The dog was sleeping under the table again.

_____ 8. It is getting rather warm in here.

_____ 9. Ben will tell another funny story.

_____ 10. She will be traveling around Scandinavia.

Exercise 27

Rewrite the following phrases to show an incomplete action or one in progress. Retain the tense of the original phrase.

1. we study _____

2. she has learned _____

3. no one speaks _____

4. I had taken _____

5. you are _____

6. it becomes _____

7. they will argue _____

8. Mark is _____

9. he drank _____

10. I write _____

11. it started _____

12. you have followed _____

13. time goes _____

14. we shared _____

15. I will dress _____

16. she will have swum _____

17. the children were _____

18. we have gone _____

19. Tina was _____

20. he spent _____

An incomplete action can often be the result of an interruption. This can occur in the present tense but is more likely to happen in other tenses.

Incomplete Action	Interruption
I was taking a bath	when the phone rang.
She had been washing the dishes	when the lights went out.
You will be sleeping	when I get home tonight.

If the incomplete action of the sentence is in the past, the verb in the interruption must be a past tense verb. If the incomplete action of the sentence is in the future, the verb in the interruption must be a present tense verb.

Exercise 28

Fill in the blank with the appropriate form of the word in parentheses. For example:

She is _dancing_ (dance) with Mark.

1. The women were _____ (play) cards when the pizza _____ (arrive).

2. Someone has _____ (be) eating cake.

3. We had been _____ (relax) in the yard when the rain _____ (start).

4. I _____ (be) trying on my clothes.

5. When Mr. Thomas _____ (arrive), I _____ (be) still taking a nap.

6. We are _____ (sit) in the den and _____ (read).

7. When the storm _____ (begin), we _____ (be) hiking in the woods.

8. I will _____ (be) working in the basement when you _____ (come) home.

9. You _____ (have) been fixing that car for hours.

10. The girls are _____ (pretend) that they are astronauts.

11. Jim was _____ (write) a letter when his sister _____ (burst) into his room.

12. I will _____ (be) preparing supper when the TV news program _____ (begin).

13. Marie _____ (be) taking two summer school courses.

14. Last year she _____ (be) taking one course but soon dropped it.

15. Bob has _____ (be) living at our house since last June.

6

Questions and Verbs

Yes-No Questions

Questions are statements that inquire into or ask about someone or something. When you ask a question that can be answered by either yes or no, there are two ways to form the question. In one of these ways, if the verb in the sentence is a form of **to be**, the verb precedes the subject in a present or past tense question.

> **Statement:** He **is** at work today.
> **Question: Is** he at work today?
> **Answer:** Yes, he is at work today. No, he is not at work today

> **Statement:** The boys **were** in Boston.
> **Question: Were** the boys in Boston?
> **Answer:** Yes, the boys were in Boston. No, the boys were in Philadelphia.

Because the incomplete or progressive form of a verb is composed of a form of **to be** plus a present participle, the same question structure is used in the present and past tenses. Present participles are composed of the infinitive of a verb and the suffix **-ing** (**going, being, having,** and so on). Because it is the verb **to be** that is conjugated in this structure, a form of the verb **to be** begins the question in the present and past tenses of the progressive form. The choice of the present participle does not affect the word order.

> **Are** you having a good time?
> **Is** your brother traveling in Spain?

> **Was** I snoring too loudly?
> **Were** the children playing in the street?

Exercise 29

Rewrite each statement as a **yes-no** question.

1. We were in Germany last summer.

_____

2. She is giving a speech in San Diego.

_____

3. I am certain that I am right.

_____

4. Someone was tampering with the lock.

_____

5. My nephew is serving in the Air Force.

_____

6. Mr. Kelly was shoveling snow in the driveway.

_____

7. These pants are too tight.

_____

8. You were being very stubborn again.

_____

9. I am thinking of staying another week in Denver.

_____

10. It was difficult to understand.

_____

11. It was storming the night he was born.

_____

12. She is my wife and my best friend.

_____

13. They were the first of our friends to become citizens.

_____

14. It is finally getting warm again.

_____

15. John was dancing with Bill's wife.

_____

If the transitive verb **to have** is the verb in question, it is often possible to structure a question in which the verb precedes the subject.

> **Statement:** She **has** a lot to do.
> **Question: Has** she a lot to do?
>
> **Statement:** You **had** enough money.
> **Question: Had** you enough money?

Do, Does, and *Did*

When a verb other than **to be** or **to have** is in a present or past tense **yes-no** question, a different structure is required. The auxiliary **to do** is the first element of the question, followed by the subject and the verb. The tense and number of **to do** are determined by the tense and number of the verb in the statement.

> **Statement:** He likes his new job.
> **Question: Does** he like his new job?
> **Answer:** Yes, he likes his new job. No, he does not like his new job.
>
> **Statement:** The men play cards every night.
> **Question: Do** the men play cards every night?
> **Answer:** Yes, the men play cards every night. No, the men play cards once a week.
>
> **Statement:** She studied at the library.
> **Question: Did** she study at the library?
> **Answer:** Yes, she studied at the library. No, she studied at home.

It is more common to use the auxiliary **to do** with the transitive verb **to have** rather than the verb-precedes-subject structure of a question.

> **Statement:** She **has** a lot to do.
> **Question: Does** she have a lot to do?
>
> **Statement:** You **had** enough money.
> **Question: Did** you have enough money?

Exercise 30

Rewrite the following statements as questions.

1. Daniel broke the expensive, new mirror.

_____

2. I sold the little house on the lake.

_____

3. Martin brings her flowers every week.

_____

4. She loves his latest novel.

_____

5. We were swimming in Lake Michigan.

_____

6. Ms. Garcia bought a cottage in the mountains.

_____

7. Somebody knows the correct answer.

_____

8. Havana is the capital city of Cuba.

_____

9. Jim really speaks four languages.

_____

10. Ben had a problem with his car again.

_____

11. You filled out the form incorrectly.

_____

12. Her brother has her car today.

_____

13. The little boys were playing with the new pups.

_____

14. The doctor placed a cast on his broken ankle.

_____

15. They stand on the corner and chat for a long time.

_____

16. I am sick of these arguments.

_____

17. She learned of Tom's illness today.

_____

18. The river is warm enough for swimming.

_____

19. Mark builds a cabinet for his girlfriend.

_____

20. He landed the little plane in a field.

_____

The Perfect and Future Tenses

In the perfect tenses, past participles are combined with a form of the auxiliary **have**, and in the future tense, infinitives are combined with the auxiliary **will** or **shall**. In such cases, the auxiliary is the first element of a question, followed by the subject and the past participle or infinitive. For example:

> **Statement:** She **has** studied in Chicago.
> **Question: Has** she studied in Chicago?
> **Answer:** Yes, she has studied in Chicago. No, she has studied in New York.

> **Statement:** We **had** bought the house.
> **Question: Had** you bought the house?
> **Answer:** Yes, we had bought the house. No, we had not bought the house.

> **Statement:** Tom **will** travel to France.
> **Question: Will** Tom travel to France.
> **Answer:** Yes, Tom will travel to France. No, Tom will travel to Italy.

Exercise 31

Rewrite the following statements as questions.

1. Mr. Roberts had lived in Asia all his life.

_____

2. The girls will help repair the chairs.

_____

3. I have become quite ill again.

_____

4. Tina will prepare some lunch for us.

_____

5. You had already seen that movie.

_____

6. Someone has taken my glasses from my desk.

_____

7. They will arrive here by 10 P.M.

_____

8. It will be late when Mark gets home.

_____

9. Aunt Mary has gone to her country home.

_____

10. Bill had always liked your cooking.

_____

Will and Shall

In Chapter 2 you encountered the difference between **will** and **shall**. There is still one more difference to consider when using **will** or **shall** in questions when the subject is the first-person singular or plural.

The general rule is to use **shall** in questions that ask what one should do when the subject is the first-person singular or plural. However, if the subject (**I** or **we**) is wondering about what the future holds, then the appropriate future tense auxiliary is **will**. Compare the following groups of questions.

Questioning Whether This Is What One Should Do

Shall I buy a new car?

Shall I help you carry those boxes?

Shall we take a stroll down to the lake?

Shall Bill and I return the books for you?

Wondering What the Future Holds

Will I ever buy a new car?

Will I win the lottery someday?

Will we see one another again in the future?

Will Mary and I get married soon?

Exercise 32

Circle the appropriate auxiliary (**will** or **shall**) for each question. Then in the blank provided, write the number 1 if the question is asking whether one should do something. Write the number 2 if the subject in the question is wondering what the future holds.

1 = what one should do

2 = what the future holds

____ 1. Will / Shall we take a drive out into the country?

____ 2. Will / Shall I warm up some soup for you?

____ 3. Will / Shall I be rich and famous someday?

____ 4. Will / Shall you and I borrow Dad's car to go downtown?

____ 5. Will / Shall we get there on time?

____ 6. Will / Shall we drop in on Henry for a visit?

____ 7. Will / Shall I ever get accepted into Harvard University?

____ 8. Will / Shall we find the money somewhere in his house?

____ 9. Will / Shall Marie and I clean up the kitchen for you?

___ 10. Will / Shall I become a surgeon someday?

Modal Auxiliaries

Just like other auxiliaries (**be, have, do, will,** and **shall**), most modal auxiliaries are the first element in a **yes-no** question. Here are a few examples:

Can you explain this to me?

Should we get off the bus at the next corner?

Must the boys be so loud?

Were we **supposed to** donate some money?

Ought she **to have** said that?

However, certain auxiliaries used in present and past tense questions require the use of **to do** as their auxiliary verb. For example:

Do you **have to** play the piano right now?

Do they **like to** dance?

Does your father **need to** rest for a while?

Did they **used to** have a house in this neighborhood?

Did Tina **want to** go out for dinner?

Did anyone **wish to** read these old magazines?

But when the same auxiliaries are used in the perfect and future tenses, just like other verbs, **to do** is not used.

Have you **had to** study long?

Had he **wanted to** take a nap?

Will the tourists **like to** go shopping?

Exercise 33

Rewrite each phrase as a question with the modal auxiliary provided. Retain the tense of the original phrase. For example:

they learn *Do they want to learn?* (want to)

1. we lived _____ (have to)

2. he will sing _____ (be allowed to)

3. she writes _____ (like to)

4. you arrived _____ (be to)

5. someone bought _____ (be supposed to)

6. I think _____ (must)

7. we argued _____ (used to)

8. you speak _____ (ought to)

9. they will test _____ (wish to)

10. he had stayed _____ (need to)

Interrogatives

A second type of question is composed of an introductory interrogative word followed by the subject and verb. Interrogative words ask about a specific element in a sentence. For example:

Interrogative Word	Asks About
who	animate subject
whom	animate object
whose	possession by an animate subject or object
what	animate subject or object
where	location or motion to a place
when	time
which	distinction between things
how	manner or mode
why	reason or cause

The interrogative **how** can be combined with other words to form new interrogatives. Following are but a few examples:

how often	how long
how many	how soon

Verbs are generally not affected when a statement is changed to a question with an interrogative word. They follow the rules described previously for the various auxiliaries. However, the interrogatives that replace the subject of a sentence (**who** and **what**) break that rule. For example, even though the original subject of a sentence is a plural, the interrogative subject is always singular. That means that the form of the verb changes.

Who and *What* as Interrogative Words

<u>Bill</u> is a friend of hers.	<u>Who</u> is a friend of hers?
<u>The girls</u> were playing soccer.	<u>Who</u> was playing soccer? (*were* becomes *was*)
<u>Their house</u> looks beautiful.	<u>What</u> looks beautiful?
<u>The flowers</u> smell nice.	<u>What</u> smells nice? (*smell* becomes *smells*)

Other Interrogative Words

His apartment is <u>in London</u>.	<u>Where</u> is his apartment?
Bill arrived <u>at seven sharp</u>.	<u>When</u> did Bill arrive?
He had driven <u>too fast</u>.	<u>How</u> had he driven?
Mary finally met <u>Susan</u>.	<u>Whom</u> did Mary finally meet?

Exercise 34

Rewrite the following sentences as questions. Change the underlined element to the appropriate interrogative word.

1. <u>Ms. Kelly</u> has taken a trip to China.

_____

2. The <u>blue</u> tie looks better on you.

_____

3. The German tourists are traveling <u>as far as Tucson</u>.

_____

4. She cried so hard <u>because Paul cannot come home for the holidays</u>.

_____

5. We work out <u>four times a week</u>.

_____

6. <u>The farm</u> made a profit for them every year.

_____

7. He found <u>twenty gold coins</u> in an old chest.

_____

8. <u>Robert's</u> wife is a Hollywood actress.

_____

9. You can bring those boxes to me <u>today</u>.

_____

10. <u>Several paintings</u> were stolen from the museum.

_____

7

Imperatives

Both transitive and intransitive verbs can form commands—that is, they become imperatives. The base form of a verb, the infinitive, becomes an imperative when the particle word **to** is omitted. To be polite, the word **please** is often included in the command. Here are some examples:

Infinitive	Imperative
to be	Be on your best behavior.
to come	Please come home soon.
to have	Have a good time at the party.
to spend	Spend less money.
to stop	Stop fighting, please.

The subject of an imperative verb such as those just illustrated is the second-person **you**. However, that pronoun is elliptical; it is not said or written but understood. No matter what the subject of a sentence might be, when the sentence is changed to an imperative, no subject is stated. And no matter what tense the verb of a sentence has, when it is stated as an imperative, the verb is given as the base form.

John found the money.	Find the money.
We will drive to Montana.	Drive to Montana.

In the case of auxiliaries, this form of imperative cannot be used. Instead, the auxiliary follows the pronoun **you** in an ordinary sentence that suggests what someone should do.

You ought to help your father.
You should go to work on time.
You are supposed to fill out these forms.

Exercise 35

Rewrite the following sentences as imperatives. Note that the sentences are given in a variety of tenses. For example:

> We are trying to organize these files.
> *Try to organize these files.*

1. My sister came home early.

_____

2. The men will stay home from work.

_____

3. I listened to these new CDs.

_____

4. Marie has sung in a choir.

_____

5. He borrowed a lawn mower from the neighbors.

_____

6. You water the vegetable garden and the flowers.

_____

7. No one believed me.

_____

8. We are quiet.

_____

9. I went to the movies with friends.

_____

10. We had had a hamburger with fries.

_____

11. Mom turns on the lights.

_____

12. Mr. Snyder will return the books tomorrow.

_____

13. Mark stood up.

_____

14. They were sleeping in that large tent.

_____

15. You ran to the store.

_____

16. His sister kissed the children good-night.

_____

17. Your parents were smart about this.

_____

18. She hurried to the hospital.

_____

19. We looked into the mirror and were surprised.

_____

20. He will sit down and take his shoes off.

_____

Let's

Another form of English imperative infers that the person giving the command is participating in the action of the command. Imperatives of this type begin with the contraction **let's** (**let us**) and are followed by an infinitive phrase.

> Let's listen to some music.
> Let's ask to borrow Dad's car.
> Let's go to the movies tomorrow.
> Let's try not to argue so much.

Exercise 36

Rewrite the following sentences as imperatives with **let's**. Note that the sentences are given in a variety of tenses. For example:

> We buy some ice cream.
> _Let's buy some ice cream._

1. They will take a drive out to Lake Tahoe.

_____

2. Our uncle has tried to be fair about this.

_____

3. We test the soil for insects.

_____

4. We don't bother the newborn kittens.

_____

5. I wrote Karen a couple postcards.

_____

6. We are on time more often.

_____

7. You had spent a lot more time talking.

_____

8. She forgot about the problems with the car.

_____

9. Tom arranged for a taxi.

_____

10. Mr. Snyder gets home before sunset.

_____

11. Earn some extra money.

_____

12. Marie and I went out dancing.

_____

13. Donate some money to their cause.

_____

14. I will join an athletic club.

_____

15. His brothers were more helpful.

_____

16. Who practiced kicking goals?

_____

17. Are we planning our winter vacation?

_____

18. Take the bus to town.

_____

19. Jim has bathed that smelly dog.

_____

20. Were you renting an apartment in the city?

_____

Let

If the verb **let** is used without the contraction of **us** (**let's**), it still is an imperative, but it has a different meaning. It suggests that someone or something is allowed to perform an action. The verb **let** is followed by a direct object and an infinitive phrase.

> Let me help you with that.
> Let us know whether you can come for a visit.
> Please let the problem just go away.
> Let the players get a little rest, please.

Negation

When negating most imperatives, **do not** or its contraction **don't** become part of the command.

Command to *You*

Do not open the door.	Don't open the door.
Do not be late.	Don't be late.
Do not have any cake.	Don't have any cake.

Command with *Let*

Do not let him sit there.	Don't let him sit there.
Do not let the game start without me.	Don't let the game start without me.

The exception to this rule is **let's**. The negative adverb **not** is placed after the contraction **let's**.

> Let's not worry about that.
> Let's not leave the house today.
> Let's not be so angry.

Exercise 37

Rewrite the following sentences as imperatives with **let**. Note that the sentences are given in a variety of tenses. For example:

> John sells his old car.
> *Let John sell his old car.*

1. The soldiers stopped under a shady tree.

2. My father has not given them more money.

3. I recommend a good restaurant to you.

4. She asked for a raise.

5. The lawyers have agreed on the selling price.

6. When did Mark explain it to you?

7. Doesn't some other person work on this job?

8. They made a list of their complaints.

9. He pretends he doesn't know us.

10. It happens naturally.

11. The balloons have floated into the sky.

_____

12. He is captain of the team.

_____

13. Does her husband do it for her?

_____

14. I have to change my clothes.

_____

15. That was a warning to you.

_____

16. The dogs slept in the garage.

_____

17. They had worn some funny costumes.

_____

18. Anna will help with the puzzle.

_____

19. I had answered.

_____

20. Will your friend lend you the money?

_____

General Commands

Imperatives also occur in general commands. These commands are usually given as announcements (over a loudspeaker, for example) or are written as signs (such as on a wall). Some examples:

Keep moving. (_what a police officer tells a crowd_)
Keep to the right. (_a sign along a highway_)
No smoking. (_a sign on a wall_)
No talking. (_a sign in a library_)
Pick up your order here. (_a sign at a restaurant drive-up window_)
Place your order here. (_a sign at a restaurant drive-up window_)
Please line up alphabetically. (_a sign in a school; an announcement_)

Reduce speed ahead. (*a sign along a highway*)

Remain behind the yellow line. (*a sign at a passport checkpoint*)

Wait your turn. (*a sign in a business office or store*)

Exercise 38

In the blank provided, write the number 1 if the sentence is a standard imperative with the pronoun **you** receiving the command. Write the number 2 if the imperative includes the speaker in the action. Write the number 3 if the imperative suggests that someone or something is allowed to perform the action. Write the number 4 if the imperative is a general command.

_____ 1. Stay in your line until called.

_____ 2. Please send me your latest catalog.

_____ 3. Let's have a surprise party for Martin.

_____ 4. Have a wonderful time on your vacation.

_____ 5. Get out!

_____ 6. Fasten your seatbelts.

_____ 7. Let the students correct their own work.

_____ 8. Hold on tight.

_____ 9. No loitering.

_____ 10. Give me a dozen donuts, please.

_____ 11. Let it rain.

_____ 12. Let's not get something to eat.

_____ 13. Take good care of your little sister.

_____ 14. Try to hold your breath for two minutes.

_____ 15. Fly the Friendly Skies.

_____ 16. Let's bet on it.

_____ 17. Share the candy with your brothers.

_____ 18. Let me try to repair that chair.

_____ 19. Don't follow me, please.

_____ 20. Pull your car over to the curb, sir.

8

Negation and Contractions

To Be

When a form of the verb **to be** is negated in the present or past tense, the adverb **not** follows the verb. This is true even when the verb **to be** is part of a longer phrase or an auxiliary.

> This is **not** my coat.
> We are **not** allowed to play in that room.
> I am **not** feeling well today.
> My sister was **not** at school today.
> They were **not** very good friends.

When an auxiliary is used with a form of the verb **to be**, the adverb **not** stands between the auxiliary and the verb. This is true with auxiliaries that change the tense (**have**, **had**, **will**, and **shall**) and modal auxiliaries.

> This has **not** been a very good day.
> Mary had **not** been here before.
> I shall **not** be able to attend your party.
> This will **not** be my first time in America.
> You can**not** be wrong again.
> We ought **not** to be so sure that we are right.
> I had better **not** be late for class.

If a sentence that contains a form of the verb **to be** or an auxiliary is in question form, the adverb **not** will follow the subject of the sentence.

> Are you **not** Marie's brother?
> Was Tim **not** at the movies last night?
> Have they **not** repaired the car yet?
> Should you **not** get a little rest?

This same structure occurs when a question begins with an interrogative word.

Why are they **not** at home yet?
What could he **not** understand?

Do, Does, Did

When the transitive verb **to have** is negated in the present and past tenses, the adverb **not** sometimes follows the verb. However, this form is not the most commonly used.

I have **not** any money.   I had **not** a car.

The more common way of negating the verb **to have** as well as most other verbs is by placing a form of the verb **to do** plus **not** before the verb. The tense and number of the positive sentence determines the tense and number of the verb **to do**.

Positive	**Negative**
I have a book.	I **do not** have a book.
He has money.	He **does not** have money.
We had a lot of time.	We **did not** have a lot of time.

The same format is used with other verbs.

Positive	**Negative**
She spells well.	She **does not** spell well.
I caught the ball.	I **did not** catch the ball.
They like this novel.	They **do not** like this novel.
They brought a bottle of wine.	They **did not** bring a bottle of wine.

Because the other tenses require the use of an auxiliary and auxiliaries follow the rules previously described, a form of **to do** is not used in the perfect or future tenses.

Present: We do not live there.
Past: We did not live there.
Present Perfect: We have not lived there.
Past Perfect: We had not lived there.
Future: We will not live there.

In the present and past tenses, a question that is negated begins with a form of the verb **to do** and the adverb **not** follows the subject of the sentence. In the perfect and future tenses, the question begins with the auxiliary and the adverb **not** follows the subject.

> **Do** you **not** understand what I mean?
> **Does** the doctor **not** know about your illness?
> **Did** I **not** tell you to be home on time?
> **Have** they **not** been here before?
> **Had** she **not** signed the document?
> **Will** the men **not** work today?

If an interrogative word begins a question, a form of **to do** follows the interrogative word and **not** follows the subject in the present and past tenses. In the other tenses, an auxiliary follows the interrogative word.

> What **did** she **not** hear?
> Whom **have** they **not** visited?

Exercise 39

Rewrite the following sentences by placing **not** in the appropriate position. Add a form of **to do** where necessary.

1. Mike spoke with the landlord.

   _____

2. I held open the door.

   _____

3. We will arrive on time.

   _____

4. Lightning strikes the tree.

   _____

5. Will your father help us?

   _____

6. Jim will travel by train.

   _____

7. I like hiking in the rain.

   _____

8. Mary has broken her arm.

_____

9. Had they lived here long?

_____

10. You should buy a house in town.

_____

11. Our vacation went by too fast.

_____

12. He has kept the money for himself.

_____

13. You write very well.

_____

14. The children have been learning French.

_____

15. Your voice sounds angry.

_____

16. I saw them at the store.

_____

17. What did you sell?

_____

18. Shall I serve dinner?

_____

19. They come from Cuba.

_____

20. Jean sent her a postcard.

_____

Other Negatives

There are several other words that can negate a sentence. For example:

I have **no** money. (*an adjective*)
We **never** visited them. (*an adverb*)
No one saw us hiding. (*a pronoun*)
Nobody bought any tickets. (*a pronoun*)
Nothing is that important. (*a noun*)
The bus went **nowhere** interesting. (*an adverb*)

Some of these negative words have a counterpart that is composed of the adverb **not** and a word with the prefix **any-**. One form is simple negation; the other form is complex negation.

Simple Negation	Complex Negation
no	not any
no one	not anyone
nobody	not anybody
nothing	not anything
nowhere	not anywhere

Both forms can negate a sentence but in different ways. The form that uses **not any-** requires a form of the verb **to do** in the present and past tenses except if the verb in the sentence is a form of **to be** or an auxiliary.

Simple Negation	Complex Negation
He bought **no** shoes.	He **did not** buy **any** shoes.
I dance with **no one**.	I **do not** dance with **anyone**.
She saw **nobody**.	She **did not** see **anybody**.
I have **nothing** for you.	I **do not** have **anything** for you.
We found them **nowhere**.	We **did not** find them **anywhere**.

These examples illustrate these forms of negation in other tenses and with other auxiliaries:

Simple Negation	Complex Negation
He is **nowhere** to be found.	He **is not anywhere** to be found.
We have found **no one**.	We **have not** found **anyone**.
They will ask for **nothing**.	They **will not** ask for **anything**.
You must have **no** conscience.	You **must not** have **any** conscience.

Exercise 40

Rewrite the following phrases with the **not any-** form of negation.

1. She sees no one. _____
2. Has he found nothing? _____
3. They are going nowhere. _____
4. Tom hurts nobody. _____
5. We lost no time. _____
6. I believe no one. _____
7. This is nothing. _____
8. They got nowhere. _____
9. I had questioned nobody. _____
10. They will receive no gifts. _____

Let's and *Let*

The imperative forms **let's** and **let** use two different types of negation. The adverb **not** follows **let's**. The verb **do** plus **not** precede **let**.

> Let's **not** argue about that.
> Let's **not** go out for dinner tonight.
> Let's **not** get up too early tomorrow.

> **Do not** let Jim work on the car.
> **Do not** let me forget to take my purse.
> **Do not** let the children play in the living room.

Contractions

It is common to write verbs and **not** together as one word—as contractions. Compare the following pairs of phrases.

Verb plus *not*	Contraction
is not	isn't
was not	wasn't
have not	haven't
cannot	can't
shall not	shan't
should not	shouldn't

Exercise 41

Rewrite the following verb phrases as contractions.

1. would not _____

2. must not _____

3. is not allowed _____

4. could not _____

5. will not _____

6. had not _____

7. need not _____

8. were not _____

9. have not been _____

10. will not be _____

11. does not _____

12. did not _____

13. was not able to _____

14. were not supposed to _____

15. are not _____

When contractions are formed with words other than **not**, the contraction is negated by following it with the adverb **not**.

I **am** not	I'm not
you **will** not	you'll not
you **are** not	you're not

Exercise 42

Rewrite the following verb phrases as contractions that are followed by the adverb **not**.

1. they have not _____

2. we are not _____

3. it is not _____

4. I would not _____

5. she will not _____

6. you have not _____

7. Sarah is not _____

8. you would not _____

9. he is not _____

10. they will not _____

In a statement, **not** is in the same position as is a contraction with **not**.

He is not at home.   He isn't at home.
They will not help.   They won't help.
She has not arrived yet.   She hasn't arrived yet.

But in a question, **not** follows the subject, whereas a contraction with **not** is attached to the auxiliary.

Is he not at home?   Isn't he at home?
Will they not help?   Won't they help?
Has she not arrived yet?   Hasn't she arrived yet?

Exercise 43

Rewrite the following sentences by placing **not** in the appropriate position and by adding a form of **to do** where necessary. Use a contraction wherever possible.

1. Laura danced with the landlord.

_____

2. I held her hand.

_____

3. We will depart on time.

_____

4. The boys are asleep.

_____

5. Can your father help us?

_____

6. I will travel by bus.

_____

7. Do you like playing the guitar?

_____

8. The boy has broken his arm.

_____

9. Had he worked here long?

_____

10. You would buy a car from him.

_____

11. Can they go to the store?

_____

12. She has kept the puppy warm.

_____

13. You sing very well.

_____

14. They have been learning about Mexico.

_____

15. That song sounds sad.

_____

16. He saw them yesterday.

_____

17. We bought it from Mr. Garcia.

_____

18. She did it wrong.

_____

19. Dad must try to bake a cake.

_____

20. I should speak with her.

_____

9

Modifying Verbs

Verbs are modified by adverbs. Adverbs can be individual words, phrases, or clauses. And there is more than one type of adverb. They are adverbs of frequency, manner, time, place, and degree.

Most adverbs are formed by adding the suffix **-ly** to an adjective while conforming to the English rules of spelling (for example, **-y** changes to **-i** = **happily**).

Adjective	**Adverb**
careful	carefully
quick	quickly
simple	simply

A few adverbs are identical to their adjectival counterparts. For example:

Adjective	**Adverb**
early	early
fast	fast
late	late
monthly	monthly
daily	daily
weekly	weekly
yearly	yearly

Adverbs of Frequency

When a transitive verb is modified by an adverb of frequency, the adverb tends to stand in front of the verb unless the adverb is in the form of a phrase. Then it comes at the end of the sentence. Adverbs of frequency answer the question *how often*.

She **usually** buys her clothes at this store.
I **sometimes** like waffles with whipped cream.
The women **rarely** have enough time.
They come home **once a week**.

If the verb phrase includes an auxiliary, the adverb of frequency follows the auxiliary.

I have **sometimes** liked waffles with whipped cream.
The women will **rarely** have enough time.

Adverbs of Manner

Adverbs of manner tend to follow an intransitive verb or verb of motion. Adverbs of manner answer the question *how*.

Martin will drive **slowly**.
She runs **excitedly** into the room.
I am walking **briskly**.

Adverbs of manner can be individual words or phrases. Let's look at some of these.

Individual Words	**Phrases**
badly	with great sadness
politely	in anger
calmly	with a happy smile

An adverb of manner has more than one position in a sentence when it modifies a transitive verb. It can sometimes introduce the sentence, it can stand before the verb, or it can stand at the end of the sentence. For example:

Gently he kissed her cheek.
He **gently** kissed her cheek.
He kissed her cheek **gently**.

If the adverb is in the form of a phrase, it is not placed before the verb.

With a big smile on my lips, I opened my gifts.
I opened my gifts **with a big smile on my lips**.

Exercise 44

Rewrite the following sentences in the tenses shown in parentheses. Change the adverb of frequency in bold to another adverb of frequency of your choice.

1. (Present) I **never** spend my money wisely.

(Past) _____

(Present perfect) _____

(Future) _____

2. (Present) She **seldom** sits with me.

(Past) _____

(Present perfect) _____

(Future) _____

3. (Present) Bob **rarely** writes me.

(Past) _____

(Present perfect) _____

(Future) _____

Follow the same directions. But change the adverb of manner in bold to another adverb of manner of your choice.

4. (Present) He rushes home **out of breath**.

(Past) _____

(Present perfect) _____

(Future) _____

5. (Present) She speaks the words **softly**.

(Past) _____

(Present perfect) _____

(Future) _____

6. (Present) They turn the corner **fast**.

(Past) _____

(Present perfect) _____

(Future) _____

Adverbs of Time

Adverbs of time—such as **now, still, yesterday, finally,** or **Monday**—answer the question *when.* They can be individual words, phrases, or clauses. For example:

Individual Words	**Phrases**	**Clauses**
recently	on Friday	after the dance ended
today	during the week	since she left home
tomorrow	in the winter	before he got on the train

Adverbs of time can introduce a sentence or follow it.

Yesterday, he bought a new laptop.
He bought a new laptop yesterday.

During the day, Bob began to feel ill.
Bob began to feel ill during the day.

Exercise 45

Circle the adverb that should appear in the blank to appropriately modify the verb in the phrase.

1. she _____ worries (late / previously / rarely / in the morning)

2. I have _____ sung (never / last year / twice a week / someday)

3. they arrived _____ (seldom / usually / early / December)

4. _____ he began his story (with a little grin / fast / tomorrow / never)

5. _____ I'll help (fast / angrily / today / kindly)

6. he went there _____ (on his bike / formerly / closely / when you leave)

7. we _____ enjoyed ourselves (always / daily / in the evening / yesterday)

8. you said that _____ (next week / only once / never / in a month)

9. _____ we stayed here (in a day / during summer / quickly / calmly)

10. they will _____ participate (last year / gladly / in the fall / last Monday)

11. he had run _____ (never / formerly / fast / when I phone)

12. we _____ have a party (rudely / slowly / often / in the spring)

13. I have _____ seen that (quickly / last week / yesterday / seldom)

14. it broke _____ (yesterday / after she arrives / soon / before I sing)

15. it happened _____ (with a loud bang / next Friday / calmly / until 5 A.M.)

Adverbs of Place

Adverbs of place answer the question *where*. Some of these adverbs are single words.

anywhere	somewhere
here	there
inside	underground
overseas	upstairs

Other adverbs of place appear in phrase form, primarily as prepositional phrases.

near the window	at home
in the kitchen	on the table
alongside the highway	over there

Adverbs of place tend to follow the verb. Let's look at some example sentences.

They lived **overseas** for two years.
I help mom **in the kitchen**.
We were painting **downstairs**.
They now live **in Buffalo**.

Exercise 46

In the blank provided, write the letter *T* if the adverb in bold is an adverb of time. Write the letter *P* if the adverb is an adverb of place.

_____ 1. Al was reading **in the garden**.

_____ 2. I met Susan **at a party**.

_____ 3. She lost her gloves **while she was running**.

_____ 4. The train left the station **late**.

_____ 5. My room is **upstairs.**

_____ 6. There is something **under the rug.**

_____ 7. This program is broadcast **locally.**

_____ 8. The dog is always kept **outside.**

_____ 9. Do you have a house **around here?**

_____ 10. My wallet fell **behind the dresser.**

_____ 11. I tried to contact you **on Tuesday.**

_____ 12. Let's stay **out on the patio.**

_____ 13. You had better phone me **in the morning.**

_____ 14. I want to meet your sister **soon.**

_____ 15. She spent the summer **abroad.**

Adverbs of Degree

Adverbs of degree answer the question _to what extent_ something is done. Some of these adverbs are:

adequately	practically
almost	profoundly
entirely	quite
extremely	rather
greatly	really
highly	too
perfectly	very

These adverbs help to define other adverbs that modify verbs.

She spoke **extremely** rapidly.
She spoke **very** rapidly.
She spoke **too** rapidly.

He answered her **almost** rudely.
He answered her **extremely** rudely.
He answered her **practically** rudely.

Exercise 47

Circle the adverb that should appear in the blank to appropriately modify the adverb in the sentence.

1. She shouts _____ loudly. (gladly / extremely / calmly / profoundly)

2. I worked _____ carefully. (finally / weekly / rather / early)

3. The door opened _____ slowly. (soon / afterward / rudely / really)

4. They have visited _____ often. (highly / too / immediately / in winter)

5. Dinner was served _____ on time. (almost / perfectly / afternoon / early)

6. He danced _____ well. (at home / rather / recently / regularly)

7. She paints _____ beautifully. (daily / rarely / greatly / quite)

8. You speak _____ honestly. (too / there / anywhere / with a grin)

9. I understood you _____ clearly. (perfectly / greatly / highly / late)

10. He patted the puppy _____ gently. (usually / home / at home / extremely)

Using Participles

English participles come in two forms: present participles and past participles. Each form has its own unique function when part of a verb phrase. But both can be used in the same way when functioning as modifiers.

Present Participles

A present participle is formed by adding the suffix **-ing** to the infinitive of a verb while conforming to the English rules of spelling (for example, **-e** is omitted = **make** → **making**). Some examples:

talking	finding
being	discussing
hurrying	shaking

A present participle is used with a form of **to be** to form the progressive or incomplete tense of a verb.

I am singing.
She was learning.
They have been appearing.
What had been happening?
You will be driving.

Exercise 48

Rewrite the following phrases in the tenses shown in parentheses.

1. (Present) Who is speaking?

(Past) _____

(Present perfect) _____

(Future) _____

2. (Present) I am going home.

(Past) _____

(Present perfect) _____

(Future) _____

3. (Present) Are you helping?

(Past) _____

(Present perfect) _____

(Future) _____

4. (Present) Marie is crying.

(Past) _____

(Present perfect) _____

(Future) _____

5. (Present) The children are playing.

(Past) _____

(Present perfect) _____

(Future) _____

Although present participles are formed from verbs, they can be used to modify nouns. If the present participle is used alone, it can precede the noun it modifies. If the present participle is part of a longer phrase, it follows the word it modifies.

the **sitting** girl	the girl **sitting here**
a **sleeping** puppy	a puppy **sleeping under the table**
the **laughing** man	the man **laughing at her joke**

Adverbs can modify verbs. Therefore, if an adverb modifies the present participle, the phrase can precede the noun or follow it.

a **calmly** sleeping puppy	a puppy **calmly** sleeping
the **loudly** laughing man	the man **loudly** laughing

This function of present participles is used in place of relative clauses. For example:

The girl **who is sitting**.	The **sitting** girl.
The boys **who are playing ball**.	The boys **playing ball**.

A present participle is also used when the verb in the relative clause is in the habitual or complete form.

The girl **who sits**.   The **sitting** girl.
The boys **who play ball**.   The boys **playing ball**.

Exercise 49

Change the phrase that contains a relative clause to one that uses the present participle as a modifier. If the present participle can be located in two positions, write the phrase in two forms.

1. a woman who is napping _____

2. the cat that chases a mouse _____

3. the top that is spinning _____

4. a team that is winning again _____

5. a story that develops _____

6. the boys who read _____

7. a student who is studying hard _____

8. a river that runs through the valley _____

9. snow that is gently falling _____

10. music that fills my ears _____

11. something that puzzles me _____

12. the waves that are loudly crashing _____

13. the waves that crash on the beach _____

14. rain that is filling the streets _____

15. flowers that slowly bloom _____

16. someone who yells a lot _____

17. a book that costs more than twenty dollars _____

18. the class that is rather boring _____

19. people who exaggerate everything _____

20. storms that are destroying homes _____

Past Participles

Regular past participles are formed by adding the suffix **-ed** to the verb, while conforming to the English rules of spelling (for example, **-y** changes to **-i-** = **hurry** → **hurried**). Regular participles are identical to the simple past tense. Irregular participles are formed in a variety of ways, often with a vowel change in the stem of the verb and an **-en** ending. Let's look at some commonly used irregular past participles.

Infinitive	Past Participle
to go	gone
to have	had
to speak	spoken
to cut	cut

Look at the appendix for a list of irregular past participles.

A past participle is used to form the present perfect, past perfect, and future perfect tenses.

	Regular Verb	Irregular Verb
Present Perfect	he has looked	he has stolen
Past Perfect	he had looked	he had stolen
Future Perfect	he will have looked	he will have stolen

Exercise 50

Rewrite the following infinitives as past participles.

1. to spell _____
2. to write _____
3. to sell _____
4. to happen _____
5. to see _____
6. to say _____
7. to fit _____
8. to watch _____
9. to please _____
10. to find _____

11. to help _____

12. to control _____

13. to develop _____

14. to send _____

15. to make _____

16. to show _____

17. to bring _____

18. to know _____

19. to think _____

20. to be _____

Exercise 51

Rewrite the following phrases in the tenses shown in parentheses.

1. (Present perfect) Who has spoken?

(Past perfect) _____

(Future perfect) _____

2. (Present perfect) I have taught.

(Past perfect) _____

(Future perfect) _____

3. (Present perfect) She has been.

(Past perfect) _____

(Future perfect) _____

4. (Present perfect) You have broken.

(Past perfect) _____

(Future perfect) _____

5. (Present perfect) We have slept.

(Past perfect) _____

(Future perfect) _____

Although past participles are formed from verbs, they can be used to modify nouns. If the past participle is used alone, it can precede the noun it modifies. If the past participle is part of a longer phrase, it follows the word it modifies.

the **broken** chair	the chair **broken during our move**
a **rented** cottage	a cottage **rented for the summer**
recorded voices	voices **recorded by the police**

Adverbs can modify verbs. Therefore, if an adverb modifies the past participle, the phrase can precede the noun or follow it. If the phrase follows the noun, the adverb has two positions in the phrase.

the **recently** broken chair	the chair **recently** broken / broken **recently**
poorly recorded voices	voices **poorly** recorded / recorded **poorly**

This function of past participles is used in place of passive voice relative clauses. For example:

the man **who was injured**	the **injured** man
the book **that was read by him**	the book **read by him**

The same thing occurs when the passive verb in the relative clause is the progressive or incomplete form.

the house **that was being razed**	the **razed** house
the poem **that was being written in French**	the poem **written in French**

However, it is possible to use the progressive form of the verb as a modifier by placing **being** in front of the past participle. But this form can only follow the noun.

The poem **being written in French**.

(The passive voice will be taken up in detail in Chapter 18.)

Exercise 52

Change the phrase that contains a relative clause to one that uses the past participle as a modifier. If the past participle can be located in more than one position, write the phrase in its various forms.

1. the apple that was eaten by Jack _____

2. the word that was written _____

3. people who were arrested _____

4. a girl who was kissed by him _____

5. a church that was being built in the city _____

6. music that was heard throughout the house _____

7. a room that was painted red _____

8. the car that was being repaired _____

9. the barn that was set on fire _____

10. the movie star that was much photographed _____

11. the bedroom that was richly decorated _____

12. the child that was gently placed on the bed _____

13. the operation that was being successfully completed _____

14. a car that was buried by the snow _____

15. leaves that were carelessly burned _____

16. shoes that were just polished _____

17. candy that was being eaten _____

18. a village that was reached only by air _____

19. the vehicles that were stopped _____

20. film that was developed slowly _____

11

Verbals: Infinitives and Gerunds

Infinitives and gerunds are called verbals; they are derived from verbs but do not function as verbs.

Infinitives

Infinitives are the base form of a verb that is preceded by the particle word **to**: **to run, to sing, to play**, and so on. An infinitive may function as a subject, a direct object, a subject complement, an adjective, or an adverb in a sentence.

When an infinitive is used as the subject of a sentence, it is functioning as a noun.

Infinitive as Subject	**Noun as Subject**
To wait makes me angry.	Your laziness makes me angry.
To run is great exercise.	A brisk walk is great exercise.

An infinitive can be used as any of the following:

- The direct object of a sentence

    I always liked **to study**.
    Everyone wanted **to participate**.

- The subject complement of a sentence

    Her greatest joy is **to dance**.
    Robert's wish was **to fly**.

- An adjective

    No one had the courage **to disagree**.
    They receive a message **to surrender**.

- An adverb

> We must practice **to win**.
> You cannot just think **to understand**.

Exercise 53

In the blank provided, write the letter *S* if the infinitive in bold is used as the subject of the sentence. Write the letter *D* if it is used as the direct object. Write the letter *C* if it is used as the subject complement. Write the letters *AJ* if it is used as an adjective. Write the letters *AV* if it is used as an adverb.

_____ 1. John never liked **to sing**.

_____ 2. Why do you want **to leave**?

_____ 3. You have to study **to learn**.

_____ 4. The best exercise to me is **to jog**.

_____ 5. **To play** video games can be a waste of time.

_____ 6. **To fall** in love can be dangerous.

_____ 7. She always hated **to gossip**.

_____ 8. They get the command **to attack**.

_____ 9. That is a cruel thing **to do**.

_____ 10. **To lie** was his own choice.

Infinitives are used very commonly in infinitive phrases. That is, they are combined with other elements such as adverbs, objects, or prepositional phrases. Infinitive phrases are used in the same way as individual infinitives. For example:

> **To smoke anywhere in this building** is prohibited. (*subject*)
> Bill agreed **to give me a ride to work**. (*direct object*)

There are several transitive verbs that can be followed by infinitive phrases. Some of the most commonly used are:

agree	begin	continue	decide
fail	hesitate	hope	intend
learn	neglect	offer	plan
prefer	pretend	promise	refuse
remember	start	try	

Here are some example sentences:

> They **begin** to understand his problem.
> I **hope** to visit Europe someday.
> The men **planned** to work on the old car.

Often a noun or pronoun precedes an infinitive phrase and functions somewhat like the subject of the infinitive phrase. That phrase can then be used as a direct object in a sentence.

> My boss asked **me** to organize an office party.
> I wanted **the children** to spend more time reading.

There are several transitive verbs that are followed by a subject and infinitive phrase. Some of the most commonly used are:

advise	allow	convince	remind
encourage	force	hire	teach
invite	permit	tell	appoint
order			

Here are some example sentences:

> We never **allowed** him to use our car.
> Ms. Garcia **teaches** the children to read.
> No one **told** me to wash the dishes.

Exercise 54

Complete each sentence with an infinitive phrase formed from the words in parentheses. For example:

> She asks . . .
> (John / speak English)
> She asks _John to speak English_.

1. I wanted . . .

   a. (they / hurry home) _____

   b. (you / help wash the car) _____

   c. (someone / find a solution) _____

    d. (she / dance with me) _____

    e. (Bill / fix the bicycle) _____

2. Jim asks . . .

    a. (I / lend him ten dollars) _____

    b. (we / drive him home) _____

    c. (he / come for dinner) _____

    d. (the girls / meet him in an hour) _____

    e. (no one / join him) _____

3. Mom reminded . . .

    a. (she / return by noon) _____

    b. (they / eat a good lunch) _____

    c. (Tom / set his alarm clock) _____

    d. (you / buy some milk) _____

    e. (Mark and Sue / stay in their rooms) _____

4. Mr. Brown will hire . . .

    a. (we / sort the mail) _____

    b. (she / type some letters) _____

    c. (I / work in the warehouse) _____

    d. (the men / repair the furnace) _____

    e. (he / clean the office) _____

The transitive verbs **to ask, to expect, to want,** and **would like** can be used with an infinitive phrase that has a subject or that has none. For example:

> Bill asks **me** to go to the library with him.
> Bill asks to see my stamp collection.

> I expected **Mary** to be on time.
> I expected to find you at home today.

> I don't want **it** to happen again.
> I don't want to lose any more money.

> Would you like **us** to stop by for a visit?
> Would you like to go shopping?

Exercise 55

Complete each sentence with two infinitive phrases formed from the words in parentheses. Write one with the subject provided; write one without the subject. For example:

> She asks . . .
> (John / speak English / dance with me)
> She asks *John to speak English.*
> She asks *to dance with me.*

1. Do you expect . . . ?

   a. (they / come here every day) _____

   b. (receive a good salary) _____

2. Someone asked . . .

   a. (I / pay you a visit) _____

   b. (use my laptop) _____

3. We would like . . .

   a. (she / apply for the job) _____

   b. (introduce them to our son) _____

4. I don't want . . .

   a. (anyone / use my credit card) _____

   b. (stay here very long) _____

Gerunds

Gerunds are verbals that look like present participles. Present participles are used to form progressive tenses or as modifiers. Gerunds, however, are used as nouns that describe an action or a state of being. Compare how a gerund can be used in the same way as any other noun.

Gerund as Noun	Standard Noun
Running keeps me fit.	**Exercise** keeps me fit.
I like **swimming**.	I like **music**.

Gerunds can be used like other nouns: as a subject, a direct object, a subject complement, or an object of a preposition.

Baking takes a lot of talent. (*subject*)

Do you really like **ironing**? (*direct object*)

What I'm best at is **wrestling**. (*subject complement*)

The boy was punished for **lying**. (*object of preposition*)

Exercise 56

In the blank provided, write the letter *S* if the gerund in bold is used as the subject of the sentence. Write the letter *D* if it is used as the direct object. Write the letter *C* if it is used as the subject complement. Write the letter *P* if it is used as the object of a preposition.

_____ 1. I never cared for **singing**.

_____ 2. **Joking** is out of place here.

_____ 3. My pet peeve was **gossiping**.

_____ 4. None of us is interested in **programming**.

_____ 5. The activities run from **jogging** to oil painting.

_____ 6. Is **talking** allowed in the library?

_____ 7. The next skill she wants to learn is **flying**.

_____ 8. **Snoring** really irritates me.

_____ 9. I always save a little time for **napping**.

_____ 10. Have you tried **painting**?

_____ 11. I have always enjoyed **knitting**.

_____ 12. **Drinking** can harm your health.

_____ 13. Her eyes were red from **crying**.

_____ 14. Why don't you like **diving**?

_____ 15. His worst habit had been **speeding**.

Just as infinitives can appear in phrase form, so, too, can gerunds. They can be accompanied by direct objects, indirect objects, adverbs, and prepositional phrases. For example:

Writing **a theme** is difficult for me. (*direct object*)

Giving **her** the money was a bad idea. (*indirect object*)

Talking **too loudly** got me in trouble. (*adverbs*)

We always liked sitting **on the porch in the evening**. (*objects of prepositions*)

Because gerunds function as nouns, they can be modified by possessive adjectives. Do not confuse the use of pronouns that are modified with present participles with gerunds that are modified by possessive adjectives.

Present Participle as Modifier	Possessive and Gerund as Noun
He saw me **running** up the hill.	The coach likes my **running**.
I watch Jane **acting**.	He's proud of her **acting**.
I heard them **singing**.	Their **singing** needs some work.
Speaking quietly, she gave them the news.	Your **speaking** quietly will keep him calm.

Exercise 57

Complete each sentence with two gerund phrases formed from the words in parentheses. Write one with the noun or pronoun provided as a possessive adjective; write the second one without the possessive adjective. For example:

She likes . . .
(I / to sing and dance / to sleep late)
She likes *my singing and dancing.*
She likes *sleeping late.*

1. Bill heard . . .

   a. (you / to complain about the food) _____

   b. (to snore at night) _____

2. We really admire . . .

   a. (she / to be so courageous) _____

   b. (to try to give up smoking) _____

3. Do you enjoy . . . ?

   a. (John / to joke about such things) _____

   b. (to stroll through the park) _____

4. I hate . . .

   a. (they / to gossip about me) _____

   b. (to work in such humidity) _____

5. Tina would prefer . . .

   a. (we / to visit on another day) _____

   b. (to travel to South America) _____

6. We really loved . . .

    a. (he / to act in that play) _____

    b. (to spend time with you) _____

7. No one liked . . .

    a. (Mary / to punish the boys so much) _____

    b. (to drink the stale tea) _____

8. I would choose . . .

    a. (you / to cook any day) _____

    b. (to remain here for the week) _____

9. Why did you dislike . . . ?

    a. (I / to chat with Jim) _____

    b. (to wear your new suit) _____

10. Mom is so proud of . . .

    a. (she / to be promoted) _____

    b. (to win the lottery) _____

12

Subject-Verb Agreement

Choosing a singular verb for a singular subject or a plural verb for a plural subject is called *agreement* and is generally simple. Because most verbs, except those that follow a third-person singular subject, are identical in the present tense, it is only the third-person singular subject that has to be identified in order to apply the appropriate ending (-s).

Pronoun	to learn	to have
I	learn	have
you	learn	have
he / she / it	<u>learns</u>	<u>has</u>
we	learn	have
they	learn	have

Only the verb **to be** is more complex, and certain auxiliaries require no ending changes at all. For example:

Pronoun	to be	must
I	am	must
you	are	must
he / she / it	is	must
we	are	must
they	are	must

Certain kinds of subjects require a bit more thought when determining subject-verb agreement.

Verbs and Indefinite Pronouns

Indefinite pronouns are used like other third-person singular pronouns but do not refer to any person or thing in particular. These pronouns begin with four prefixes: **any-, every-, no-,** and **some-.**

anybody	everybody	nobody	somebody
anyone	everyone	no one	someone
anything	everything	nothing	something

Compare their use with personal pronouns.

He is here.	*replaces* **John** is here.
She went home.	*replaces* **Her aunt** went home.
It belongs to me.	*replaces* **This hat** belongs to me.
They helped out.	*replaces* **My sons** helped out.

Does **anybody** want this?	**anybody** *refers to no specific person*
Everyone had a good time.	**everyone** *refers to all the people but none specifically*
Nothing is perfect.	**nothing** *refers to no specific object*
Someone here is a thief.	**someone** *refers to no specific person but suggests that the thief is among those* here

Because an indefinite pronoun is a third-person singular pronoun, it must be used with third-person singular possessive adjectives. Use **his** when referring to males and **her** when referring to females. **Its** is the possessive adjective required for inanimate objects.

Indefinite Pronoun	Possessive Adjective
anyone	his / her
everything	its
nobody	his / her
something	its

However, it is very common in informal English to use the possessive adjective **their** in place of **his** or **her**.

Formal	Informal
Someone lost **his / her** book.	Someone lost **their** book.
No one brought **his / her** laptop.	No one brought **their** laptop.

This informal usage does not occur with **anything, everything, nothing,** and **something,** which refer to inanimate singular objects and always use the possessive adjective **its.**

Everything has lost **its** meaning.
We found something. **Its** shape is very odd.

Exercise 58

Complete the second sentence in each pair with the correct possessive adjective, based upon the content of the first sentence. Conjugate the verb in parentheses in the second sentence appropriately. For example:

> The men are in a crowded room. Someone should (to give) _give his_ seat to the
> oldest man.

1. All the girls are here. But no one _____ _____ (to have) ticket along.

2. She calls the meeting to order. Everyone _____ _____ (to lower) voice.

3. The men are quiet. Yet every one of them _____ _____ (to hear) heart beating.

4. Something falls on the floor. _____ color _____ (to be) bright red.

5. Someone took my jacket! And _____ name _____ (to be) Jack!

6. Is there anything in the corner? I _____ hear _____ (can) breathing.

7. She asks the boys for their names. But nobody _____ _____ (to provide) ID.

8. How strange. But I suppose everyone _____ _____ (to have) own way of doing things.

9. I called to the girls. "Somebody _____ _____ (to leave) purse here."

10. The teacher stood at the door. Everyone _____ in _____ (to hand) test upon leaving.

When a second clause follows a clause with an indefinite pronoun in it, the second clause requires a singular verb with a third-person singular pronoun.

> Someone will get in trouble if **he / she is** dishonest.
> I have something you'll like, and **it is** made of chocolate.
> Anybody **who** says that **he / she understands** this formula is lying.

Complete each relative clause in any appropriate way. Provide a possessive adjective in your clause.

1. I know no one who _____.

2. Have you met anybody who _____?

3. Everyone who _____ can board the plane now.

4. I can't find anyone who _____.

5. Let's ask somebody who _____.

Verbs and Collective Nouns

Some collective nouns describe a single entity doing the same thing and must be used with a third-person singular verb. A collective noun's pronoun replacement is **it** and its possessive adjective is **its**.

> They have a nice **family**.   **It** is quite large.

But in formal style, when a collective group does individual things, a plural verb is required as well as the use of **they** and **their**.

> Their **family** took separate vacations. **They** went **their** own ways for a month.

Compare these sentences:

One Group Doing the Same Thing	**Individuals in the Group Acting Alone**
The **choir sings** beautifully.	The **choir are** fitted with **their** new robes.
(*one entity*)	(*the choir members*)

However, it is more common in American English not only to use a singular verb with this kind of collective (where individuals in the group act alone) but to use a plural pronoun and possessive adjective as well. For example:

> The **choir is** fitted with **their** new robes.
> The **team quits** early and **goes** to **their** homes.
> The **class was** asked to pick up **their** new books.
> The **faculty is** told that **they** each must prepare three tests.

Following are some commonly used collective nouns:

army	firm
audience	group
board	jury
cabinet	majority
class	minority
committee	navy
company	public
corporation	school
council	senate
department	society
faculty	team
family	troupe

Exercise 60

Circle the word in parentheses that best completes each sentence.

1. The crowd _____ cheering for the team. (is / are / were)

2. Our swim team _____ very good although rather small. (is / are / be)

3. The audience clapped loudly. _____ loved the play. (it / they / its)

4. The orchestra is provided with _____ new formal wear. (its / his / their)

5. The navy announced that _____ had sunk the pirate ship. (they / it / her)

6. A majority _____ in favor of the new law. (are / were / is)

7. The jury _____ hear the witness. (don't / doesn't / are able to)

8. The large family now lives in _____ own house. (it / its / their)

9. The company has lost _____ contract with the city. (it / its / their)

10. Which department _____ going to be eliminated? (are / is / will)

Verbs and Noncount Nouns

There is a group of nouns that cannot be counted or named either singular or plural. Such nouns are noncount nouns; in general, they describe a collective or an intangible concept. Although the meaning of such nouns can describe a large quantity of something, they use a third-person singular verb. The nouns can be identified by checking their use with the article **a / an.** If they cannot be used with the indefinite article, they are noncount nouns.

> Used with a definite article: **The furniture** looks a bit old.
> Used with no article: We need to buy **furniture.**
> Makes no sense with *a*: Where is **a furniture?** (*furniture is a noncount noun*)

The following list contains many of the most frequently used noncount nouns:

air	homework
anger	leisure
bread	meat
corn	precision
courage	progress
dust	reading
education	smoke
electricity	software
equipment	steam
fish	sugar
furniture	warmth
gravity	weather
hate	wood

Exercise 61

In the blank provided, write the appropriate present tense conjugation of the verb in parentheses with the subject provided.

1. fish _____ (to have)

2. precision _____ (to be)

3. water _____ (ought to)

4. gravity _____ (to form)

5. software _____ (to be)

6. dust _____ (to make)

7. smoke _____ (to carry)

8. air _____ (to become)

9. meat _____ (must)

10. courage _____ (to need)

Verbs, Complex Nouns, and Quantities

Complex nouns are composed of a noun combined with a subordinate noun by use of the preposition **of.** For example:

a bottle of water   the book of matches   two cups of coffee

When complex nouns are used as the subject of a sentence, the agreement of the verb is determined by the initial noun (singular or plural) and not the subordinate noun.

Singular	**Plural**
A glass of water is . . .	Four glasses of water are . . .
One bottle of wine has . . .	Several bottles of wine have . . .

However, if the complex noun expresses a single quantity, the verb is singular. If the complex noun implies that a quantity is composed of individual units, the verb is plural.

Four cups of sugar (*in a single bowl*) **is** the correct amount.
Four cups of sugar (*in four different cups*) **are** needed.

Other words that express quantities must be looked at carefully when determining whether a singular or plural verb is required. Some of these are as follows:

Singular Verb Required
each of
either one of
every one of
much of
one of
one-fourth of (*or other fraction*)
the number of

Plural Verb Required
a number of
many of

Singular or Plural Verb Can Be Used
most of
none of (*the plural form is considered casual or informal*)

some of

three-fourths of (*or other fraction*)

Here are some examples:

Each of the men **receives** an award.
One-fourth of the students **earns** a bad grade.

Many of our ideas **are** considered bad.
A number of the delegates **votes** "no."

Most of her money **is** in the stock market.
Some of the girls **have to** buy new shoes.

Three-fourths of the test **is** multiple choice.
Three-fourths of the students **are** getting good grades.

Exercise 62

Complete the following phrases with the present tense of the verb **to be**.

1. each of you _____

2. either one of the boys _____

3. a spoonful of sugar _____

4. two cups of flour _____

5. none of them _____

6. most of the food _____

7. most of the girls _____

8. a tank of gas _____

9. three-tenths of a yard _____

10. some of the tourists _____

Follow the same directions using the verb **to have**.

11. some of his money _____

12. many of your friends _____

13. a number of cities _____

14. a fifth of the work _____

15. one of these children _____

16. much of their time _____

17. a bowl of soup _____

18. most of the day _____

19. many of you _____

20. none of the above _____

Follow the same directions using the verb **to do.**

21. most of it _____

22. the number of hours _____

23. each of us _____

24. four pints of blood _____

25. one of the guests _____

26. either of the sisters _____

27. a pad of paper _____

28. some of them _____

29. some of the article _____

30. both of your friends _____

There Is / There Are

The use of **there is / there are** is idiomatic and is synonymous with *there exists.* The noun or pronoun that follows this expression determines the number of the verb. If the noun or pronoun is singular, the verb is singular. If it is plural, the verb is plural.

> There **is** someone here to see you. (*singular pronoun*)
> There **is** a mouse in the corner. (*singular noun*)
> There **are** many reasons for his failures. (*plural noun*)

This expression can be used in all the tenses and with a variety of auxiliaries.

Past: There was a problem with the car.

Present Perfect: There have been numerous complaints.

Past Perfect: Had there been any improvements?

Future: There will be a meeting tomorrow.

Auxiliary: There can be no more discussion about this.

Exercise 63

Circle the verb that best completes each sentence.

1. There _____ a few questions for you. (is / are / was)

2. There _____ anyone to help us. (am not / wasn't / weren't)

3. _____ there any more objections? (Is / Are / Wasn't)

4. How many kinds of cat breeds _____ there? (is / are / has been)

5. There _____ laws against that. (are supposed to be / ought to be / has been)

6. There _____ some candy in that bowl. (are / am / was)

7. Why _____ there so many mistakes made? (is / was / were)

8. I think there _____ someone hiding over there. (wasn't / have been / is)

9. There _____ a new menu posted tomorrow. (will be / had been / has been)

10. There _____ some kind of error. (has to / weren't / must be)

13

Tenses, Number, and Clauses

Conjunctions make no sense when standing alone. Their function is as connectors. When words, phrases, or sentences are combined by conjunctions, the choice of the tense and number of the verb in the sentence is sometimes affected.

Verbs and Coordinating Conjunctions

Coordinating conjunctions are among the most commonly used and function with all the tenses. These conjunctions are:

and
but
for
nor
or
so
yet

When combining clauses that contain a subject and a verb, the tense of the verb in one clause is often the same in the other clause.

Jack works in London, and Mary works in New York.
The boys will stay home, but the girls will go to the park.
I was worried about them, so I went to the police station.

It is also possible to use a different tense in each clause to specify at what point in time the action of the verb has taken place, is taking place, or will take place.

Jack <u>is working</u> in London now, and Mary <u>will go</u> to New York to work there.
The boys <u>are</u> at home, but the girls <u>have</u> already <u>gone</u> to the park.
I <u>worry</u> about them, so I <u>will go</u> to the police station for help.

Exercise 64

Rewrite the underlined clause in each sentence in the tenses provided in parentheses.

1. I don't worry about her, yet, of course, <u>she has some problems</u>.

(past) _____

(present perfect) _____

(past perfect) _____

(future) _____

2. <u>The room gets cold</u>, so I light a fire in the fireplace.

(past) _____

(present perfect) _____

(past perfect) _____

(future) _____

3. She puts on a sweater, <u>for the temperature is changing</u>.

(past) _____

(present perfect) _____

(past perfect) _____

(future) _____

4. The children like playing outside, <u>but the weather is turning cold</u>.

(past) _____

(present perfect) _____

(past perfect) _____

(future) _____

5. She has no job <u>and is looking for work</u>.

(past) _____

(present perfect) _____

(past perfect) _____

(future) _____

6. The soccer team plays on Saturday, <u>but the golf tournament is on Friday</u>.

(past) _____

(future) _____

7. I don't like your behavior, <u>nor do I approve of it.</u>

(future) _____

8. Do you want to go to the movies, <u>or did you see that film?</u>

(present perfect) _____

(past perfect) _____

When certain coordinating conjunctions combine subjects, the choice of a singular or plural present tense verb must be considered. With the conjunction **and**, a plural present tense verb is used. With **or** and **but not**, the noun or pronoun closest to the verb determines the number of the verb. For example:

> **Plural Verb**
> John and I **are**
> two men and a little boy **have**
>
> **Singular or Plural Verb**
> a boy or a girl **is**
> the men or the women **are**
> a winner or a loser **has**
> three girls or two boys **have**
> not Tom but Tina **is**
> the father but not his children **are**
> the teachers but not the student **has**
> not the banks but the post offices **have**

Exercise 65

Complete the following phrases with the present tense of the verb **to be**.

1. several girls and I _____

2. not Jim but Karen _____

3. a group of tourists and their guide _____

4. Mr. Jones or Ms. Jones _____

5. the husband but not the wife _____

6. not the parents but the children _____

7. our neighbors and our landlord _____

8. not the red car but the blue one _____

9. my relatives or my friends _____

10. a ballerina or a singer _____

11. one lion and three tigers _____

12. one horse or three cows _____

13. four chairs or one table _____

14. not the meat but the fish _____

15. the piano or the organ _____

Verbs and Correlative Conjunctions

Correlative conjunctions comprise more than one word, and those words must function together to make sense. The five correlative conjunctions are:

> both . . . and
> not only . . . but also
> either . . . or
> neither . . . nor
> whether . . . or

Except for **both . . . and**, when you combine singular and plural subjects with these conjunctions, it is the subject nearest to the verb that determines whether a present tense verb must have a singular or plural ending. For example:

Plural Verb
Both William and Jean **live** in that building.
Both our brothers and our sisters **like** life in the big city.

Singular or Plural Verb
Not only Joe but also Helen **is** a friend of mine.
Not only the boys but also the girls **are** helping out.

Either Mary or Bill **has** your wallet.
Either the teacher or the students **have** caused the problem.

Neither the dog nor the cat **is** allowed in the living room.
Neither the dog nor the cats **are** in the basement.

Whether my son or my daughter **goes** to college is not up to me.

Whether my son or my daughters **go** to the prom is not up to me.

Verbs and Subordinating Conjunctions

There are numerous subordinating conjunctions. They combine a subordinating clause with a main clause. Unlike the main clause, a subordinating clause cannot stand on its own and make sense. Subordinating conjunctions introduce a clause that describes when the action of the verb takes place, the cause of the action, opposition to the action, and conditional action. Commonly used subordinating conjunctions include the following:

When	Cause	Opposition	Condition
after	because	although	if
before	since	though	unless
when(ever)	now that	even though	only if
while	as	whereas	whether (or not)
since	in order that	while	even if
until	so		in case that

When you use conjunctions that describe when an action occurs, the same tense is used in both the subordinating clause and the main clause if that tense is a form of the past tense.

After you went to school, I hurried to the store.

Before he had become a doctor, he worked in a drugstore.

I waited on the corner until a bus finally came.

If the present tense is used in the subordinating clause, either the present or the future tense will occur in the main clause.

When you come home, you always do your homework.

Mom takes a nap while the children are at school.

Before he leaves the house, Tom must have a good breakfast.

Until he makes his bed, my son will not be allowed to watch television.

When **since** means "from that time," it is used only in the past tense.

Since I met you, I've learned so much about music.

Exercise 66

Circle the word or phrase that is the best completion for each sentence.

1. Whenever I _____ out late, I regret it the next day. (have been staying / stay / will stay)

2. Tina _____ the door after Bill gets home. (will lock / has locked / locked)

3. Until the weather changes, you _____ remain in the house. (did / will have to / had)

4. Bob _____ in Florida before he found a job in Denver. (works / will work / had been working)

5. Since Mary _____, we have scarcely spoken to one another. (arrives / will arrive / arrived)

6. We will be sitting in the garden while you _____ supper. (prepare / will prepare / will be preparing)

7. When the door opens, you _____ your new apartment. (saw / have seen / will see)

8. After I shower, we _____ go down to breakfast. (did / can / will)

9. I didn't know what happiness was until I _____ you. (am meeting / will meet / met)

10. Before I give you the money, I _____ you to sign this. (have wanted / want / was wanting)

Conjunctions that introduce a clause that describes the cause of an action can contain a variety of tenses, particularly when the verb in the main clause is in the present tense.

> You are afraid because you are in a new situation.
> You are afraid because you already had problems with him.
> You are afraid because you will have to confront him over this.

> I am happy, so I celebrate with a friend.
> I have enough money, so I have decided to take a vacation.
> I don't like this job, so I will look for a new one.

If the verb in the main clause is in the past tense or the future tense, the tense varieties in the subordinating clause are limited to the past tense and the present tense respectively, especially in clauses introduced by **in order that** and **now that**.

> Mom was delighted now that Tim decided to go to college.
> We will give him some money in order that he can get on his feet.

Exercise 67

Circle the word or phrase that is the best completion for each sentence.

1. I have been lonely since you _____ me anymore. (don't visit / didn't visit / visit)

2. Because you _____ a friend, I will not ask for an apology. (are / was / will have been)

3. Mary began to cry, so he _____ ashamed. (has been / felt / had not felt)

4. Dad is going back to work now that his health _____ good. (was / will be / is)

5. He just gave up as there _____ little he could do. (was / will be / was being)

6. We will visit you in order that we _____ you face-to-face. (see / have seen / saw)

7. Since you lost your job, you _____ borrow money from us. (must have / have to / could have)

8. She trusted you because you _____ a loyal friend. (will be / hadn't been / were)

9. My stomach aches, so I _____ to the doctor. (was going / will go / had gone)

10. Now that the war _____ over, we can get on with our lives. (has been / was / is)

When you use conjunctions that describe **opposition**, the verbs in both the subordinating clause and the main clause can appear in a variety of tenses.

> Even though I have little money, I will buy some new clothes.
> Even though I had little money, I bought some new clothes.
> Even though I will have little money, I will buy some new clothes.

With conjunctions that set a prerequisite or condition, the verb in the main clause is in the present or future tense, and the verb in the subordinating clause is in the present tense.

> We will dine here only if you join us.
> You cannot go to the concert unless you clean your room.

Exercise 68

Circle the word or phrase that is the best completion for each sentence.

1. Although the weather _____ warmer, we are going home tomorrow. (is turning / becomes / wasn't)

2. I _____ a new cabin only if you help me. (could build / will build / built)

3. If you are good, I _____ home a surprise for you. (bring / am bringing / will bring)

4. While your words are kind, your voice _____ stern. (was / is / will be)

5. John loves jazz, whereas Mike _____ it. (will play / heard / hates)

6. Whether or not she approves, I _____ to the concert. (went / am going / have been going)

7. Unless you pay your rent, you _____ your apartment. (will lose / had lost / lost)

8. She _____ here even if her sister moves out. (lived / has lived / will live)

9. Though it _____ hard to believe, I passed the test. (is / was / will be)

10. Even though he _____ me, he will not marry me. (loves / is loving / was loving)

11. I _____ here even if you pay me double. (don't work / won't work / haven't worked)

12. Although he _____ I'm right, he insists I'm wrong. (will know / knows / can know)

13. If that _____ true, then Mark is lying to me. (is being / was being / is)

14. Though I can't believe you, I _____ believe you. (am wanting to / want to / will want to)

15. He will stay at his present job unless he _____ into college. (gets / will get / was getting)

16. Sarah is the brightest, whereas Tom _____ the strongest. (was / is being / is)

17. I will come home only if you _____ me. (ask / asked / will ask)

18. While having this job was important, going to school _____ more important. (is / was / is being)

19. These are the facts whether or not you _____ them. (are understanding / understand / understood)

20. Even if Bob _____ the team, we still can't win. (joins / was joining / had joined)

14

The Verb *Get*

There are few verbs in English that have the variety of meanings and uses as the verb **to get**. It has an irregular conjugation.

Pronoun	Present	Past	Present / Past Perfect	Future
I	get	got	have / had gotten	will get
you	get	got	have / had gotten	will get
he / she / it	gets	got	has / had gotten	will get
we	get	got	have / had gotten	will get
they	get	got	have / had gotten	will get

The **to get** verb is frequently used to mean "receive," "obtain," or "acquire."

I just got a letter from Bill. (*received*)
It's difficult to get information from them. (*obtain*)
She got her reputation by being honest. (*acquire*)

To get can also be used to show that someone has had the quality or condition of a person or an object altered or improved.

I got the car repaired.
We need to get the house repainted.
You have to get my father well again.

Similarly, the same verb is used to show that someone provokes another person into a certain action.

I'll get Mr. James to sign the petition.
You should get your father to lend you the money.

And **to get** can be used as a synonym for *to become*.

It's getting rather cold.

It is also a synonym for *to arrive* or *to go*. It is usually accompanied by a prepositional phrase introduced by **to** or **from**.

> I got to the hospital on time.
> We have to get to my sister's house.

Exercise 69

Circle the word or phrase that best completes each sentence.

1. Why did you get _____ with me? (the weather / angry / so brilliantly)

2. Tom got _____ from Mary. (another letter / a bit warmer / soon)

3. Let's get the car _____. (buying / to sell / washed)

4. Our room is getting _____. (some gifts / nothing / rather hot)

5. When did you get _____? (your new car / from Bill / later)

6. John never gets _____ in time for supper. (right away / home / work)

7. I should get _____. (for the children / my hair trimmed / after school)

8. When will we get _____? (the TV repaired / us / the airport)

9. How can I get _____ to understand the problem? (a letter / something / you)

10. How did they get _____? (for us / to the hotel / of the train)

11. Jane has gotten _____. (a strange package / where / boredom)

12. I couldn't get _____ to lend me the truck. (in the office / my boss / those machines)

13. We will get _____ by tomorrow. (teams / uninteresting / an answer)

14. I always get _____ at holiday time. (chilly / arranged / happy)

15. Somehow Tim got _____. (for the concert / a new passport / polished)

16. I have to get _____. (these documents filed / my new dentist / by taxi)

17. We should get _____ in an hour. (on time / at home / to Toronto)

18. I got _____. (after the play / a note from her / anybody)

19. You'll never get _____ to agree. (the book / anything / her)

20. Get _____! (about your parents / pleasantly / to your room)

To get can mean that someone can supply or furnish another person with something.

> I'll get you a ticket to the concert.
> Can you get me a can of soda, please?

When it is followed by an infinitive or infinitive phrase, it means that someone is allowed or given the opportunity to do something.

> If you're good, you'll get to go to Uncle Bill's house.
> No one got to see the play.

Followed by a direct object, it can infer that someone is puzzled or irritated by another person or thing.

> His bad behavior really gets me!
> Your awful language got mother.

And **to get** is sometimes used as a synonym for *to understand*.

> Don't you get it?
> That man will never get what I said.

When the past tense of **to get** is combined with **to have**, it becomes an emphatic form of **must** or **to have to** and is followed by an infinitive or infinitive phrase.

> I have got to start working on my taxes.
> Tina has got to end her fear of flying.

When the same structure is followed by a direct object, its meaning is an emphatic form of **to have**.

> He has got a book of mine.
> Have you got any time to help me?

Exercise 70

In the blank provided, write the letter of the phrase that describes how **to get** is used in each sentence.

> A. synonymous with *supply* or *furnish*
> B. *have the opportunity*
> C. *puzzle* or *irritate*
> D. synonymous with *understand*
> E. emphatic form of *must*
> F. emphatic form of *have*

_____ 1. We have got to go to work on time.

_____ 2. I think I can get those books for you.

_____ 3. That awful speech really got me.

_____ 4. Has Mary got the magazines she promised us?

_____ 5. I don't get you.

_____ 6. The boys hope they get to go on the hike.

_____ 7. My family never got to go to Disneyland.

_____ 8. Try to get us some good seats at the ball game.

_____ 9. I don't think Mr. Cane got the joke.

_____ 10. You have got to stop biting your nails.

_____ 11. John hasn't got enough money.

_____ 12. That little boy has got to try harder in school.

_____ 13. Do you know anyone who would get the meaning of this?

_____ 14. Mom has gotten me a new pair of shoes.

_____ 15. What did they get you for your birthday?

_____ 16. That sudden kiss got her.

_____ 17. Dad will get you something to eat.

_____ 18. They have just got to see that movie.

_____ 19. We haven't got enough time for this.

_____ 20. I wanted to get to know the new girl from Chile.

Get, Adverbs, and Prepositions

The verb **to get** is often combined with adverbs and prepositions to form new meanings. Some of the most commonly used expressions are:

> to get across (to) = _to convince, to make understood_
> to get ahead = _to prosper, to be successful_
> to get along (with) = _to cooperate, to try to be friends_
> to get at = _to hint, to find out_
> to get away (with) = _to succeed at an unwanted or a criminal act_
> to get by = _to succeed with little effort_
> to get in = _to arrive_

to get over = *to recover*
to get together (with) = *to meet, to assemble*
to get up = *to wake up, to rise from sleep*

Exercise 71

Using the subject provided, write each infinitive phrase in the tenses shown.

1. (I) to get the meaning across to them.

Present _____

Past _____

Present Perfect _____

Future _____

2. (they) to never get ahead.

Present _____

Past _____

Present Perfect _____

Future _____

3. (the boys) to get along well.

Present _____

Past _____

Present Perfect _____

Future _____

4. (she) to get at the source of the problem.

Present _____

Past _____

Present Perfect _____

Future _____

5. (who) to get away with a crime?

Present _____

Past _____

Present Perfect _____

Future _____

Exercise 72

Circle the word or phrase that describes how **to get** is used in each sentence.

1. The young family is trying to get ahead. (supply / prosper / become)

2. It got very cold yesterday. (succeed at a criminal act / irritate / become)

3. Mark never gets my jokes. (understand / find out / make understood)

4. We never get to go anywhere. (have the opportunity / cooperate / emphatic have)

5. She has got to stop complaining! (prosper / emphatic must / succeed with little effort)

6. Our train got in very late. (become / receive / arrive)

7. I can get you that for less money. (understand / recover / furnish)

8. What time do I have to get up? (receive / convince / wake up)

9. I have never gotten along with Bob. (cooperate / understand / make understood)

10. She finally got her brother to help her. (provoke someone to act / assemble / arrive)

11. How do we get there from here? (hint / go / succeed at a criminal act)

12. Have you got any aspirin? (succeed with little effort / emphatic have / become)

13. Let's get together with them. (meet / furnish / emphatic must)

14. When did they get their new bikes? (receive / prosper / succeed with little effort)

15. You'll never get by on your salary. (irritate / convince / succeed with little effort)

16. I just can't get over losing my job. (emphatic must / recover / have the opportunity)

17. I don't understand. What are you getting at? (convince / hint / have something done)

18. I got Jim to join the team. (provoke someone to act / prosper / emphatic must)

19. You should get the car washed. (have something done / cooperate / make understood)

20. His story gets stranger with every day. (emphatic have / furnish / become)

15

Verbs in Relative Clauses

Verbs of any type, of any tense, and of any number can occur in relative clauses. The subject relative pronouns of those verbs are **who, which,** and **that.**

There is a tendency to use **who** and **which** in nonrestrictive relative clauses. Such clauses provide additional information about the antecedent but are not essential to the basic meaning of the sentence.

> Our mayor, who is out of town right now, won reelection last week.
> These fabrics, which were manufactured in China, are rather cheap.

The relative pronoun **that** is used in restrictive relative clauses. Such clauses provide essential information about the antecedent.

> The man that lost the election received fewer than two thousand votes.
> He has a car that runs on ethanol.

When the antecedent to the subject relative pronoun is an entire main clause, the verb in the relative clause is always in the third-person singular.

> He fails his exams, which annoys his father greatly.
> She told only the truth, which itself is a lie.

Exercise 73

Fill in the blank with the appropriate form of the verb in parentheses. Some of the antecedents to the relative pronouns are entire main clauses.

1. The weather is awful again, which _____ (mean) we have to postpone the picnic.

2. The woman starts crying, which _____ (cause) me to blush.

3. There is no reason that _____ (be) a justification for this.

4. Mr. Garcia falls to his knees, which _____ (shock) his wife.

5. I finally point to the thief, which _____ (make) the man tremble.

6. We located a ship that _____ (sink) many years ago.

7. The men look for the treasure, which _____ (have to be) on this island.

8. He is beating the old horse, which _____ (horrify) the passersby.

9. They buy the paintings, which _____ (be) almost priceless.

10. Jean receives an award, which _____ (bring) her parents to tears of pride.

11. We spent the night in a motel, which _____ (be) a horrible experience.

12. I have some toys that _____ (be made) in Austria.

13. The old coat needed some buttons, which _____ (be) hard to find.

14. The little girl is sick again, which _____ (cause) her mother much pain.

15. She opens her eyes and smiles, which _____ (bring) a tear to my eye.

The possessive relative pronoun **whose** cannot stand alone as a subject. It modifies the noun subject of the relative clause, and it is that subject that determines whether a singular or plural verb is required.

> We asked the man, whose father was arrested for the crime.
> I'd like to meet the girls, whose parents want to arrange the party.

If the antecedent is an inanimate object, **of which** can replace **whose**.

> The car, whose color is red, is German.
> The car, the color of which is red, is German.

When the relative pronoun is a direct or an indirect object, or an object of a preposition, it is the subject of the relative clause that determines the verb in the relative clause.

> I recognized the man that we met at your party. (*"that" = direct object, "we met"*
>   *= subject and verb*)
> That's the lady to whom she often sends flowers. (*"whom" = object of* to, *"she sends"*
>   *= subject and verb*)

Exercise 74

Circle the verb or verb phrase that best completes each sentence.

1. The teacher, whom I _____ so much, is Ms. Allen. (knew / respect / likes)

2. That's the student that Jean _____ so much. (knew / respect / likes)

3. The fire, whose causes _____ under investigation, is under control. (was / is / are)

4. The people, whom Phillip ____ met yet, are from Ireland. (hasn't / haven't / won't)

5. The blanket, the size of which ____ too large, was returned. (was / were / are)

6. We bought the puppies, whose mother ____ become so weak. (have / wants to / has)

7. Here's the poem, which I ____ trying to understand. (are / is / am)

8. Jim collects insects that ____ rare to this region. (are / is / am)

9. I met the singer, whose brothers ____ in the band. (were / has been / is singing)

10. She cut me a piece of the cake that your sisters ____. (is baking / had baked / bakes)

11. Bob hurt his knee in the game, which ____ his poor mother. (frightens / frightened / have frightened)

12. This is the soldier, from whom we ____ e-mails. (are receiving / is receiving / receives)

13. Look at that leaf, which four ladybugs ____ sitting on. (is / wants to be / are)

14. Dad reads the newspaper that he ____ from New York. (gets / buy / have sent)

15. I lent her the novel that I ____ telling her about. (were / was / am)

When the antecedent of a relative clause describes a moment in time, a place, or a reason for an action, the relative pronouns become **when, where,** and **why.** These three relative pronouns cannot be used as the subject of the relative clause and are used adverbially. The subject will be another word in the relative clause and will determine the form of the verb.

> I recall the day when I first saw Mary. (*"I saw"* = *subject and verb*)
> This is the house where Beethoven once lived. (*"Beethoven lived"* = *subject and verb*)
> He has no explanation why this occurred. (*"this occurred"* = *subject and verb*)

Exercise 75

Fill in the blank with the appropriate word: **when, where,** or **why.**

1. I want to find a place ____ I can feel comfortable.

2. This is the kind of room ____ a pool table could be set up.

3. It was on our anniversary ____ Robert gave me some pearl earrings.

4. She has no clue ____ the refrigerator stopped working.

5. They lived in a village ____ everyone knew everyone.

6. Do you have an answer ____ you stayed out so late?

7. Tom placed his luggage on the floor in the den, ____ Mom was napping.

8. They arrived on Sunday ____ we were still at the mall.

9. There was no justification _____ she failed the test.

10. We'll meet again in the future _____ I've become a success.

11. There will be a time _____ you'll finally trust me.

12. She came to the park, _____ a rally was taking place.

13. Can you explain the reason _____ you won't come to my party?

14. It happened in January _____ the temperature was below zero.

15. They sat near the fireplace, _____ the room was the warmest.

Use **that** as the relative pronoun when the antecedent in the main clause is **all, anything, everyone, everything, few, little, many, much, nothing, none, someone,** or **something.** If **that** is used as the subject of the relative clause, the verb is generally a third-person singular, except following **all, few, many,** and sometimes **none.** If **that** is an object in the relative clause, the verb is determined by the subject of the relative clause.

That as Subject
I have spoken with all that are here. (**all** *refers to people*)
This is all that is available. (**all** *refers to a collective of objects*)
There are many that say I am wrong. (**that say** = *subject and verb*)
She has nothing that has any value. (**that has** = *subject and verb*)
We interviewed none that speak English. (**none** *refers to a group of people*)
Tom finds none that is appropriate for us. (**none** *means "not a single one"*)

That as Object
I can't find anything that you might like. (**you might** = *subject and verb*)
There is still much that we want to do. (**we want** = *subject and verb*)
John gave me something that I treasure. (**I treasure** = *subject and verb*)

Exercise 76

Rewrite the underlined relative clause of each sentence in the tenses shown.

1. There is someone <u>that you need to meet.</u>

Past: _____

Present perfect: _____

Past perfect: _____

Future: _____

2. I sold some books that are in relatively good shape.

Past: _____

Present perfect: _____

Past perfect: _____

3. She introduced Mr. Johnson, who is the chairman of the committee.

Past: _____

Present perfect: _____

Past perfect: _____

Future: _____

4. They went skydiving, which frightens me to death.

Past: _____

Present perfect: _____

Past perfect: _____

5. This is John, whose uncle lives in Mexico.

Past: _____

Present perfect: _____

Past perfect: _____

Future: _____

6. Bill preferred movies that are dubbed in English.

Past: _____

Present perfect: _____

Past perfect: _____

7. The woman gives me something that eases the pain.

Past: _____

Present perfect: _____

Past perfect: _____

Future: _____

8. This is the plot of the story that takes place in Asia.

Past: _____

Present perfect: _____

Past perfect: _____

Future: _____

9. He likes the girls who work in this store.

Past: _____

Present perfect: _____

Past perfect: _____

Future: _____

10. The lawyer, whom you meet, is Ms. Brown.

Past: _____

Present perfect: _____

Past perfect: _____

Future: _____

11. The trees, which are planted in this park, add to the beauty of nature.

Past: _____

Present perfect: _____

Past perfect: _____

Future: _____

12. We have room for all that need a ride.

Future: _____

13. They want to live in a house where there is peace and quiet.

Past: _____

Present perfect: _____

Past perfect: _____

Future: _____

14. It was on a Monday when their car broke down.

Past perfect: _____

15. It was a great victory, which makes the entire team very proud.

Past: _____

Present perfect: _____

Past perfect: _____

16

Reflexive Verbs and Reciprocal Pronouns

Reflexive Verbs

Reflexive verbs are those that have a subject and an object that refer to the same person or thing. Unlike most other European languages, English has only a few true reflexive verbs. Some examples are **absent oneself, bestir oneself,** and **perjure oneself.** These verbs make no sense unless they are accompanied by one of the reflexive pronouns that correspond to the personal pronouns.

Pronoun	Absent Oneself	Perjure Oneself
I	absent myself	perjure myself
you (sing.)	absent yourself	perjure yourself
he	absents himself	perjures himself
she	absents herself	perjures herself
we	absent ourselves	perjure ourselves
you (pl.)	absent yourselves	perjure yourselves
they	absent themselves	perjure themselves

Note: the reflexive pronoun for **it** is **itself;** the reflexive pronoun for **one** is **oneself.**

Certain other English verbs require a direct object, and if that object is the same person or thing as the subject, a reflexive pronoun is used. For example:

Direct Object	Reflexive Pronoun Object
I enjoy the party.	I enjoy myself.
He hurt the girl.	He hurt himself.

The tense of a verb does not change the use of a reflexive pronoun that accompanies it.

Exercise 77

Fill in the blank with the appropriate reflexive pronoun. Then rewrite each sentence in the tenses shown.

1. We blame _____ for the problem.

Past: _____

Present perfect: _____

Past perfect: _____

Future: _____

2. I behave _____ rather badly.

Past: _____

Present perfect: _____

Past perfect: _____

Future: _____

3. You (pl.) enjoy _____ at my party.

Past: _____

Present perfect: _____

Past perfect: _____

Future: _____

4. She doesn't control _____.

Past: _____

Present perfect: _____

Past perfect: _____

Future: _____

5. Are they washing _____?

Past: _____

Present perfect: _____

Past perfect: _____

Future: _____

6. Mary and I amuse _____ with a game.

Past: _____

Present perfect: _____

Past perfect: _____

Future: _____

7. They pride _____ on their looks.

Past: _____

Present perfect: _____

Past perfect: _____

Future: _____

8. You (sing.) guard _____ against danger.

Past: _____

Present perfect: _____

Past perfect: _____

Future: _____

9. His mother braces _____ against a chair.

Past: _____

Present perfect: _____

Past perfect: _____

Future: _____

10. I don't really like _____.

Past: _____

Present perfect: _____

Past perfect: _____

Future: _____

Many other verbs can use a reflexive pronoun as their object: a direct object, an indirect object, or an object of a preposition. Reflexive pronouns are never used as subjects.

Reflexive Pronouns as Direct Objects
I see myself in the mirror.
He found himself in a strange place.
We washed ourselves in the lake.

Reflexive Pronouns as Indirect Objects
Have you finally bought yourself a new comb and brush?
She sent herself an e-mail as a reminder.
They found themselves some good seats in the third row.

Reflexive Pronouns as Objects of Prepositions

Tom chose it as a gift for himself.

Is she talking to herself?

The guests were chatting among themselves.

Exercise 78

Combine the words provided into a sentence. Use the verb in the present tense and add a reflexive pronoun. For example:

> we / see / in the mirror
> *We see ourselves in the mirror.*

1. John / need / some medicine / for

_____

2. I / do not / permit / to smoke

_____

3. she / buy / a new dress

_____

4. they / be interested / in

_____

5. the boys / behave / so well

_____

6. why / Mary / send / flowers / ?

_____

7. you (pl.) / must lend / some money

_____

8. the professor / be thinking / to

_____

9. the players / be / proud / of

_____

10. why / you (sing.) / blame / ?

_____

11. the old man / give / a birthday present

_____

12. we / should not / speak / of

_____

13. you (sing.) / send / a reminder

_____

14. he / call / a winner

_____

15. it / raise / off the ground

_____

The action of a verb can imply that the action is carried out by the subject alone by using a reflexive pronoun. The reflexive pronoun is placed at the end of the sentence.

> She made the blouse herself. (*It was made by her alone.*)
> Jim put up the tent himself. (*It was put up by Jim alone.*)

When a reflexive pronoun follows the preposition **by**, the prepositional phrase tends to stand at the end of the sentence and means "on one's own" and "without help."

> The little boy opened the jar by himself. (*He did it on his own.*)

When the reflexive pronoun stands next to the subject, the meaning tends to be that the subject is carrying out the action of the verb "personally."

> The boss himself fired Mr. Johnson. (*The boss fired him personally.*)
> I myself identified the thief. (*I identified him personally.*)

Exercise 79

Rewrite each sentence in the past tense, and add a reflexive pronoun that shows that the action of the verb was carried out by the subject alone.

1. My brother and sister repair the car.

_____

2. We take care of the little children.

_____

3. I bake a cake.

_____

4. She struggles against the current.

_____

5. Do you (sing.) build these toys?

_____

Follow the same directions, but let the reflexive pronoun mean "on one's own."

6. The baby crawls across the floor.

_____

7. No one can survive here.

_____

8. Do they carry the heavy timbers?

_____

9. You (pl.) stack the firewood.

_____

10. My sister and I carry the suitcases.

_____

Follow the same directions, but let the reflexive pronoun mean "personally."

11. We draw up a new contract.

_____

12. I spend no money on gambling.

_____

13. Jack regrets the argument.

_____

14. Can you (sing.) take responsibility for it?

_____

15. They don't understand this illness.

_____

Reciprocal Pronouns

The reciprocal pronouns are **one another** and **each other**; the meaning of the two phrases is identical. When the subjects of two different sentences carry out the action of the same verb, the two sentences can be combined as one by means of a reciprocal pronoun. If the subjects are singular, the verbs in the two sentences are singular. But when the sentences are combined, the verb must be made plural.

John loves Mary. Mary loves John.
John and Mary **love** one another. John and Mary **love** each other.

The cat chases the dog. The dog chases the cat.
The cat and the dog **chase** one another. The cat and the dog **chase** each other.

If the verbs in the two sentences are already plural, the verb in the combined sentence remains plural.

The boys tease the girls. The girls tease the boys.
The boys and the girls **tease** one another. The boys and the girls **tease** each other.

Exercise 80

Combine the following pairs of sentences by using a reciprocal pronoun.

1. You care for me. I care for you.

_____

2. The men joke with the boss. The boss jokes with the men.

_____

3. The squirrel hides from the raccoon. The raccoon hides from the squirrel.

_____

4. Bob doesn't like Jim. Jim doesn't like Bob.

_____

5. The old elk challenges the young elk. The young elk challenges the old elk.

_____

6. I smile at you. You smile at me.

_____

7. The women don't see the men. The men don't see the women.

_____

8. His story contradicts your story. Your story contradicts his story.

_____

9. Michael helps the tourists. The tourists help Michael.

_____

10. He likes me. I like him.

_____

17

Passive Voice and Stative Passive

Passive Voice

The passive voice contains many of the same elements as the active voice. Active voice sentences that have a direct or an indirect object can be changed to the passive voice. That object becomes the subject of the passive sentence, and the active verb becomes a past participle accompanied by the auxiliary **to be**.

Active	Passive
Bill finds a wallet.	A wallet is found by Bill.
I will rent a small car.	A small car will be rented by me.

The subject of the active sentence becomes the object of the preposition **by** in the passive sentence.

Given that there are two ways to form the present and past tenses, there are two forms of the present and past tense passive voice.

the car is repaired	the car is being repaired
the book was read	the book was being read

The progressive form (the book is being read) occurs only in the present and past tenses of the passive voice.

The passive voice occurs in all tenses. For example:

Present:	the book is being read	a house is built
Past:	the book was being read	a house was built
Present Perfect:	the book has been read	a house has been built
Past Perfect:	the book had been read	a house had been built
Future:	the book will be read	a house will be built
Future Perfect:	the book will have been read	a house will have been built

Exercise 81

Rewrite each present tense passive sentence in the tenses shown.

1. The keys are lost by her.

Past: _____

Present perfect: _____

Past perfect: _____

Future: _____

2. My car is stolen by a thief.

Past: _____

Present perfect: _____

Past perfect: _____

Future: _____

3. She is being watched by someone.

Past: _____

Present perfect: _____

Past perfect: _____

Future: _____

4. Who is arrested by the police?

Past: _____

Present perfect: _____

Past perfect: _____

Future: _____

5. I am being chased by a bear.

Past: _____

Present perfect: _____

Past perfect: _____

Future: _____

6. The duck is shot by a hunter.

Past: _____

Present perfect: _____

Past perfect: _____

Future: _____

   7. The window is smashed by a rock.

Past: _____

Present perfect: _____

Past perfect: _____

Future: _____

   8. The candle is blown out by the wind.

Past: _____

Present perfect: _____

Past perfect: _____

Future: _____

   9. We are praised by our boss.

Past: _____

Present perfect: _____

Past perfect: _____

Future: _____

10. Is Laura being stopped by the guard?

Past: _____

Present perfect: _____

Past perfect: _____

Future: _____

When changing an active sentence to the passive voice, the tense of the active sentence becomes the tense of the passive sentence. For example:

Past:	He broke the mirror.	The mirror **was broken** by him.
Future:	Tom will buy the car.	The car **will be bought** by Tom.

Exercise 82

Rewrite each active sentence in the passive voice.

   1. They have taken an oath.

_____

2. Mark is watching the birds.

_____

3. I borrow her car.

_____

4. Jean will sing a song.

_____

5. The men had brought a bottle of wine.

_____

6. The mechanics were checking the engine.

_____

7. A new company published his novel.

_____

8. Did he hurt the puppy?

_____

9. Mary wrote several postcards.

_____

10. We have not painted the bedroom.

_____

11. The best students will attend this school.

_____

12. The American tourists were touring France.

_____

13. Who repaired the door?

_____

14. The professor finds something interesting.

_____

15. The landlady is opening the windows.

_____

16. He purchased a new couch.

_____

17. Bill paid the bill.

_____

18. They had not heard the new CD.

_____

19. Both of us will clean the kitchen.

_____

20. I recommended the movie.

_____

If an active sentence contains both a direct and an indirect object, either one can become the subject of the passive sentence. However, if the direct object becomes the subject of the passive sentence, the indirect object becomes the object of the preposition **to** or **for**.

Active Sentence
He gave <u>them</u> <u>a book</u>. (*"them" = indirect object, "a book" = direct object*)

Passive Sentences
They were given a book by him. (*"they" = subject*)
A book was given to them by him. (*"a book" = subject*)

Exercise 83

Rewrite the following active sentences as two passive sentences: once with the direct object as the subject and once with the indirect object as the subject.

1. Mark sends the girl a bouquet.

_____

_____

2. We have brought her some magazines.

_____

_____

3. Mr. Locke will buy each of us a candy bar.

_____

_____

4. The mayor gives me an award.

_____

_____

5. The store shipped Mary the wrong dress.

_____

_____

It is common to omit the prepositional phrase introduced by the preposition **by** in a passive sentence. This is often done to avoid mentioning who or what is carrying out the action.

Active	**Passive**
Mr. Jones fired everyone.	Everyone was fired.
He is painting two bicycles.	Two bicycles are being painted.

The omission of the phrase that follows **by** also occurs when the subject of the active sentence is some vague entity: **they, one, people, someone,** and so on.

Active	**Passive**
They grow coffee here.	Coffee is grown here.
People remember him well.	He is remembered well.

Exercise 84

Rewrite each active sentence in the passive voice and omit the phrase that follows **by**.

1. Someone threw a rock at him.

_____

2. People will never understand his poetry.

_____

3. This was causing a terrible problem.

_____

4. One took too much time.

_____

5. They had warned us before.

_____

6. That will leave a bad scar.

_____

7. People have built the houses close together.

_____

8. They visit the memorial every summer.

_____

9. Will they plant the wheat in this field?

_____

10. Some person was eating my lunch.

_____

Stative Passive

In Chapter 10 it was illustrated how past participles can be used as adjectives. The stative passive looks like the regular passive voice, but the past participle in the stative passive is used as an adjective and not as a verb. The stative passive is seen most clearly in the present or past tense or in a sentence that omits the prepositional phrase introduced by the preposition **by**. The progressive form usually indicates the passive voice is being used.

Passive Voice
The car is being repaired by Mr. Garcia.
The window was broken by our neighbor's son.

Stative Passive
The car is repaired. (*It is in a state of good repair right now.*)
The window was broken. (*The window is no longer broken.*)

To test for the stative passive, substitute a true adjective (such as **new**) for the past participle. If the sentence makes sense, the past participle is in the stative passive. For example:

The car is being **new** by Mr. Garcia. (*makes no sense*)
The window was **new** by our neighbor's son. (*makes no sense*)
The car is **new**. (*makes sense—is stative passive*)
The window was **new**. (*makes sense—is stative passive*)

Exercise 85

In the blank provided, write the letter *P* if the past participle in the sentence is in the passive voice. Write the letter *S* if the past participle is in the stative passive.

_____ 1. John was taken to the hospital in an ambulance.

_____ 2. The windows are being washed today.

_____ 3. The children were not allowed to play in the alley.

_____ 4. Bob is being fired by the new manager.

_____ 5. The flower garden is finally planted.

_____ 6. The lawn is freshly mowed.

_____ 7. We have been given two tickets to the concert.

_____ 8. The fence was being painted white.

_____ 9. Is the house painted?

_____ 10. The team will be trained by a new coach.

_____ 11. My skirt is ripped!

_____ 12. The drapes are being cleaned.

_____ 13. All my socks and underwear are washed and darned.

_____ 14. The problem was solved by a committee.

_____ 15. The cows were being herded into a pen.

Passive Voice and Modals

The future tense auxiliaries (**will** and **shall**) are followed by an infinitive in the future tense or by the infinitive **have** and a past participle in the future perfect tense.

> I shall work in the garden.
> You will not understand.
> They will have arrived by 7 P.M.

The same auxiliaries are used to form the future tense of the passive voice: **shall** or **will** followed by a passive voice infinitive (**to be** + **past participle**).

> We shall not **be harmed** by that.
> They will **be arrested**.

The passive voice is also used with other auxiliaries—the modal auxiliaries, which are followed by a passive voice infinitive (**to be** + **past participle**). (See Chapter 4 for a review of the modal auxiliaries.) Any variety of auxiliaries can be used with passive voice infinitives. For example:

To Be Found
it must be found
it could not be found
it ought to be found

To Be Helped
they can be helped
they want to be helped
they should be helped

Exercise 86

Rewrite each passive phrase with the modal provided in parentheses.

1. we are persuaded (can) _____

2. I am coached (be allowed to) _____

3. she is taught (ought to) _____

4. he is punished (had better) _____

5. you are rewarded (must) _____

6. they are fined (could) _____

7. he is guided (have to) _____

8. it is fixed (need to) _____

9. they are introduced (be supposed to) _____

10. who is elected (wish to) _____

11. they are reminded (have got to) _____

12. I am married (be to) _____

13. you are surrounded (may) _____

14. that is undertaken (might) _____

15. we are admired (used to) _____

16. it is proved (would) _____

17. she is fired (have to) _____

18. they are presented (should) _____

19. I am flattered (wish to) _____

20. he is kissed (like to) _____

Remember that it is the auxiliaries that can change tense or number, and the passive voice infinitive remains static. It does not change from its infinitive form.

> **Present:** Mary wants to be invited to the party.
> **Past:** Mary wanted to be invited to the party.
> **Present Perfect:** Mary has wanted to be invited to the party.
> **Past Perfect:** Mary had wanted to be invited to the party.
> **Future:** Mary will want to be invited to the party.

Exercise 87

Rewrite the following present tense sentences in the tenses shown. Place an X in the space where a tense change is not possible.

1. I have to be hired for the job.

Past: _____

Present perfect: _____

Past perfect: _____

Future: _____

2. You ought to be fired.

Past: _____

Present perfect: _____

Past perfect: _____

Future: _____

3. She isn't able to be reached by phone.

Past: _____

Present perfect: _____

Past perfect: _____

Future: _____

4. Can it be repaired?

Past: _____

Present perfect: _____

Past perfect: _____

Future: _____

5. You are to be commended.

Past: _____

Present perfect: _____

Past perfect: _____

Future: _____

6. That needs to be done properly.

Past: _____

Present perfect: _____

Past perfect: _____

Future: _____

7. The meat is supposed to be roasted.

Past: _____

Present perfect: _____

Past perfect: _____

Future: _____

8. The dog doesn't like to be bathed.

Past: _____

Present perfect: _____

Past perfect: _____

Future: _____

9. She wants to be dressed as a queen.

Past: _____

Present perfect: _____

Past perfect: _____

Future: _____

10. Her poems may be published.

Past: _____

Present perfect: _____

Past perfect: _____

Future: _____

Active voice sentences that contain a modal auxiliary can be changed to the passive voice. When they are, the tense and number of the modal auxiliary determines the tense and the number of the passive sentence. For example:

Active	**Passive**
She can write it.	It can be written by her.

A word of caution: Although active voice sentences that contain a modal auxiliary can be changed to the passive voice, this is not always appropriate, because the meaning and intent in the active sentence can seem awkward or even absurd in the passive sentence.

Active	**Passive**
She wanted to buy the books.	The books wanted to be bought by her. (*absurd*)
He wishes to sell the car.	The car wishes to be sold by him. (*absurd*)

This awkward or absurd meaning is apparent with inanimate subjects (**the books, the car**). But even though animate subjects make more sense with certain modal auxiliaries, the meaning of the passive sentence is not identical to the active sentence.

Active	Passive
She wanted to kiss Bill.	Bill wanted to be kissed by her.
He wishes to meet Mary.	Mary wishes to be met by him.

In the active sentences just illustrated, the subjects are showing a desire to do something: **She wanted to kiss / He wishes to meet.** However, in the passive sentences the desire to do something is attributed to the subjects of the passive sentences: **Bill wanted to be kissed, Mary wishes to be met.** With these modal auxiliaries, the meanings of the active sentence and of the passive sentence are not identical even though the sentences still make sense.

Exercise 88

Rewrite each sentence with the three modal auxiliaries provided in parentheses.

1. It cannot be done. (should, be to, must)

_____

_____

_____

2. The floor needs to be mopped. (be supposed to, ought to, had better)

_____

_____

_____

3. Mr. Peters wanted to be paid. (wish to, could, have to)

_____

_____

_____

4. Did you have to be punished? (should, would, need to)

_____

_____

_____

5. Mark doesn't like to be annoyed by his sister. (be supposed to, may, must)

_____

_____

_____

6. The problem can be solved. (be able to, need to, might)

_____

_____

_____

7. It must have been lost. (ought to have, could have, may have)

_____

_____

_____

8. This document is not allowed to be copied. (could, be supposed to, ought to)

_____

_____

_____

9. He liked to be complimented for his looks. (used to, wish to, should have)

_____

_____

_____

10. It could have been broken by your son. (must have, would, might)

_____

_____

_____

19

Subjunctive Mood

The subjunctive mood is used to express a wish, desire, supposition, contingency, or condition. The conjugations for the English subjunctive are relatively simple. The present subjunctive is formed from the infinitive of a verb, and each person has the same verb form.

Pronoun	to be	to have	to know
I	be	have	know
you	be	have	know
he / she / it	be	have	know
we	be	have	know
they	be	have	know

The past subjunctive is formed from the simple past tense of a verb, and that verb can be either regular or irregular. Each person has the same verb form.

Pronoun	to be	to have	to go	to like
I	were	had	went	liked
you	were	had	went	liked
he / she / it	were	had	went	liked
we	were	had	went	liked
they	were	had	went	liked

Note: the past subjunctive of **to be** uses only the plural **were**. The verb **was** is not used in the subjunctive conjugation.

Exercise 89

Write the present and past subjunctive forms of the verbs in parentheses with the subjects provided.

1. I _____ _____ (to help)
2. we _____ _____ (to see)
3. they _____ _____ (to make)
4. it _____ _____ (to do)

5. Michael _____ _____ (to want)

6. she _____ _____ (to be)

7. you _____ _____ (to warn)

8. the men _____ _____ (to spend)

9. he _____ _____ (to drink)

10. who _____ _____ (to laugh)

11. she _____ _____ (to have)

12. I _____ _____ (to eat)

13. he _____ _____ (to grow)

14. I _____ _____ (to be)

15. you _____ _____ (to carry)

16. we _____ _____ (to catch)

17. they _____ _____ (to allow)

18. the women _____ _____ (to be)

19. you _____ _____ (to cut)

20. he _____ _____ (to sing)

In many cases both the present and past subjunctive are identical to the present and past tenses of the indicative. The exceptions are the verbs **to be** and **to have**. For example:

Present and Past Indicative	Present and Past Subjunctive
I look / I looked	I look / I looked
we see / we saw	we see / we saw
she is / she was	she be / she were
he has / he had	he have / he had

If the indicative and subjunctive are identical, it is the usage of a verb that identifies it as subjunctive.

Present Subjunctive

The present subjunctive is used to describe the action of a verb in a clause that follows the verbs **ask, command, demand, insist, propose, recommend, request,** and **suggest.** The present subjunctive is also used when it follows a phrase that suggests what is important or necessary.

Her boss requested that she **be** on time from now on.

I suggest he **spend** more time studying.

It's important that she **begin** from the beginning once again.

Exercise 90

Look at each sentence and determine whether a present subjunctive verb is required. Then circle the verb that best completes each sentence.

1. I speak with the man who _____ across the street. (reside / lives / have bought)

2. Bob recommended we _____ this movie. (see / saw / have seen)

3. Tom suggested it _____ made a rule. (was / is / be)

4. Everyone helped the man _____ his old car. (was pushing / pushes / push)

5. The prince commanded that his servant _____ a meal. (prepare / makes / served)

6. I gave the suggestion that you _____ hired. (be / were / shall be)

7. She had to request that John _____ singing. (begins / stop / continued)

8. No one recommends that you _____ so much. (are eating / orders / drink)

9. We ask Mr. Phelps to _____ with the luggage. (help / carried / finds)

10. Everyone must _____ a bit quieter. (were / be / was)

11. I _____ recommend a good hotel nearby. (be / have / can)

12. Bill suggests Tim _____ his own problems. (solve / were / was)

13. Who requested the meeting _____ postponed? (is / have / be)

14. Ms. Walker demanded that the man _____ her purse. (steals / stole / return)

15. I must insist that he _____ with the others in the group. (were / sits / remain)

16. The lawyer proposed we _____ a new contract. (sign / arranged / are developing)

17. He asked that the judge _____ merciful. (is / be / was)

18. No one should _____ so much. (worry / be / spent)

19. The manager demanded he _____ the bill immediately. (will change / pay / charges)

20. I ask that his book _____ published. (is / were / be)

Past Subjunctive

It is common to use the past subjunctive in clauses that are introduced by **if** and **as if,** in clauses that follow a **wish-clause,** or in a clause introduced by the imperative of the verb **suppose.**

> I would be more careful if I **were** you.
> John acted as if he **understood** the poem.
> She wishes Bill **were** home from work.
> Suppose Mary **came** here now. What would you say to her?

It is possible to infer an action in the present by using the simple past subjunctive.

> She wishes he **were** home. (*now*)
> I wish you **had** good health. (*now*)

By using a verb in a perfect tense structure (**have** + **past participle**), an action in the past can be inferred.

> She wishes he **had been** home for the party. (*The party was in the past.*)
> I wish you **had had** better health then. (*"then" = a time in the past*)

This occurs with **if-clauses** as well.

> If only I **had seen** you there yesterday.

Exercise 91

Fill in the blank with the appropriate subjunctive form of the verb provided in parentheses.

1. Mary acts as if the money _____ to her. (to belong)

2. They acted as if Jim _____ a stranger. (to be)

3. I wish I _____ more money. (to have)

4. If only you _____ spend more time with us. (can)

5. Brian was smiling as if he _____ the answer. (to know)

6. Mom wishes he _____ harder last year. (to study)

7. If our daughter just _____ a little closer to us. (to live)

8. Suppose it _____ to rain. (to start)

9. If that _____ only true. (to be)

10. I always wished I _____ in America as a child. (to live)

11. The girls played as if it _____ a championship game. (to be)

12. Suppose I _____ you what she really said. (to tell)

13. If only we _____ years ago. (to meet)

14. The boy wishes he _____ a puppy. (to have)

15. Martin bragged as if he _____ English fluently. (to speak)

In sentences that contain two clauses combined by **if**, it is often the case that the subjunctive is expressed in one of the clauses by use of the auxiliary **would** and another verb. And if the imperative **suppose** introduces a sentence, it is common for it to be followed by a sentence that also uses the auxiliary **would** and another verb.

> If Bill saw this letter, he **would be** very angry.
> I **would believe** you if you hadn't lied before.
> Suppose you had a thousand dollars. What **would** you **do?**

The perfect tenses are used with these structures to infer an action that occurred in the past.

> If Bill **had seen** this letter, he **would have been** very angry.
> I **would have believed** you if you **hadn't lied** before.
> Suppose you **had had** a thousand dollars. What **would** you **have done?**

An **if-clause** sets a condition for an action in the present or past, and its accompanying clause shows the result of that action.

Condition	Result
If John were here (*now*),	he would help us (*now*).
If John had been here (*in the past*),	he would have helped us (*in the past*).

If an auxiliary is used in sentences such as these, the auxiliary is formed in the past subjunctive and the word **would** is omitted. For example:

> If John **could be** here, he **would help** us.
> If John **had been** here, he **could have helped** us.

Exercise 92

Combine the following sentences with **if** to form a subjunctive sentence that sets a condition and provides a result. For example:

> They like tomatoes. I make a salad.
> *If they liked tomatoes, I would make a salad.*

1. We are in Mexico. We go shopping every afternoon.

_____

2. You have a down payment. You can buy this car.

_____

3. The weather is better. The boys go hiking.

_____

4. My family lives in the capital. I visit the museums every day.

_____

5. The plane lands early. We can get downtown by 5 P.M.

_____

6. She catches a plane. She may be in New York by dusk.

_____

7. I understand your language. I am happy to chat with you.

_____

8. You sleep longer. You have more energy.

_____

9. The circus comes to town. We go there every day.

_____

10. Tom enjoys chess. He gladly plays with me.

_____

Rewrite the ten subjunctive sentences you have just written to infer that the action has taken place in the past. For example:

> If they liked tomatoes, I would make a salad.
> *If they had liked tomatoes, I would have made a salad.*

11. _____

12. _____

13. _____

14. _____

15. _____

16. _____

17. _____

18. _____

19. _____

20. _____

Special Expressions

There are several unique expressions that are stated in the subjunctive. Many of them are quite old, coming from a time when English used the subjunctive more extensively. Look at the following list and observe where the present and past subjunctive forms are used.

As it were, I cannot help you.

Be that as it may.

Far be it for me to criticize you.

God bless America!

(God) bless you! (*response to someone sneezing*)

God rest ye merry gentlemen . . . (*from a Christmas song*)

God save the Queen!

Heaven forbid!

I agree, come what may.

If I were you, I wouldn't do that.

If need be.

Long live the king!

So be it.

Suffice it to say, this is no solution.

The truth be told, he simply lied.

Till death do us part. (*said during marriage vows*)

Would that it were so.

Exercise 93

Circle the phrase that is the best completion for each sentence or the best response to it.

1. I hope grandfather is finally getting better. (If need be. / Would that it were so. / Heaven forbid!)

2. _____, he had been in prison twice before. (Till death do us part / Far be it for me / The truth be told)

3. You are now an American citizen! (God bless America! / If I were you. / As it were.)

4. I'm ready for anything, _____. (come what may / be that as it may / long live the king)

5. _____, I wouldn't use such language. (If I were you / If need be / Come what may)

6. _____ to try to correct your pronunciation. (Would that it were so / Far be it for me / As it were)

7. John wants to quit his job and move to Greenland. (Come what may. / Suffice it to say. / Heaven forbid!)

8. Our friendship is over. Good-bye. (So be it. / If need be. / Bless you!)

9. _____, you're the smartest student in this class. (Suffice it to say / Would that it were so / God save the queen)

10. You'll have to give up your scholarship and go to work. (If need be. / As it were. / If I were you.)

When **have** is added to certain auxiliaries, the past subjunctive meaning is understood and suggests an action that is a possibility, a desired outcome, or imaginary.

> I **could have been** a pilot.
> She **might have become** a ballerina.
> You **ought to have listened** to me.
> Laura **must have overslept** again.
> We **should have taken** the train there.

In many cases, the same phrase can be used with a variety of auxiliaries.

> It **could** have been a success.
> It **might** have been a success.
> It **ought to** have been a success.
> It **must** have been a success.
> It **should** have been a success.

Exercise 94

Rewrite the sentences with the auxiliaries provided in parentheses. Change the action to mean an action that is a possibility, a desired outcome, or imaginary.

1. I read the entire novel. (could, ought to, must)

_____

_____

_____

2. We are living in Spain. (could, might, should)

_____

_____

_____

3. Dad repairs the truck. (might, must, should)

_____

_____

_____

4. The girls memorize the poems. (could, must, should)

_____

_____

_____

5. He doesn't sell the cabin. (ought to, must, should)

_____

_____

_____

Functions of Phrasal Verbs

Phrasal verbs play a significant role in the English language. They can be identified by two characteristics: (1) a verb is accompanied by adverbs or prepositions in a phrase, and (2) the meaning of that phrase is generally quite different from the individual meaning of the words in the phrase.

For example, the verb **to come** means "arrive" or "move toward." When the verb is followed by a prepositional phrase and its meaning does not change, it is proof that it is not a phrasal verb.

Come at seven o'clock. (*Arrive at seven o'clock.*)
Come to the window. (*Move toward the window.*)

But when the meaning of the verb changes, it is a phrasal verb. For example:

He came up to the window and looked in. (*He approached the window and looked in.*)
The woman finally came to. (*The woman finally regained consciousness.*)

In these two examples, the prepositions **up** (**came up**) and **to** (**came to**) are functioning as adverbs.

There are hundreds of phrasal verbs in the English language, but only a few will be illustrated and practiced here. They will act as the pattern for other phrasal verbs.

Phrasal Verb	Meaning
to ask out	to invite for a date
to back up	to drive a car backward; to support or defend
to be in / out	to be at / away from home or in / away from the office
to drop off	to deliver
to give up (on)	to stop trying; to admit failure in a relationship or an activity
to go into	to explain; to enter a profession
to head for	to move in the direction of a place
to let on (about)	to divulge information about someone or something
to put up with	to bear, endure
to set out (on, for)	to begin a journey; to begin a journey with a destination
to take down	to write, note
to throw up	to vomit
to turn down	to refuse
to warm up to	to become gradually friendly
to write off	to give up hope on someone or something

Exercise 95

Rewrite each sentence in the tenses shown.

1. Present: Martin backs up the SUV.

Past: _____

Present perfect: _____

Future: _____

2. Present: Jim asks the new girl out.

Past: _____

Present perfect: _____

Future: _____

3. Present: Is Dr. Garcia in today?

Past: _____

Present perfect: _____

Future: _____

4. Present: They drop off a gift for the bride.

Past: _____

Present perfect: _____

Future: _____

5. Present: You never give up on me.

Past: _____

Present perfect: _____

Future: _____

6. Present: She finally goes into her reason for leaving.

Past: _____

Present perfect: _____

Future: _____

7. Present: We are heading for Alaska.

Past: _____

Present perfect: _____

Future: _____

8. Present: John doesn't let on about the surprise party.

Past: _____

Present perfect: _____

Future: _____

9. Present: Your father puts up with a lot.

Past: _____

Present perfect: _____

Future: _____

10. Present: They set out on a long journey.

Past: _____

Present perfect: _____

Future: _____

11. Present: The secretary takes down every word.

Past: _____

Present perfect: _____

Future: _____

12. Present: I always throw up on a roller coaster.

Past: _____

Present perfect: _____

Future: _____

13. Present: Barbara turns down my offer.

Past: _____

Present perfect: _____

Future: _____

14. Present: Jake slowly warms up to his boss.

Past: _____

Present perfect: _____

Future: _____

15. Present: I don't write off our team this year.

Past: _____

Present perfect: _____

Future: _____

Passive Voice

Just like other transitive verbs, phrasal verbs that are transitive can appear in the passive voice. For example:

Every comment **was taken down** in his own shorthand.
When **will** the new books **be dropped off**?
Why **are** my ideas **being written off** as worthless?

Exercise 96

Rewrite each active sentence as a passive sentence. Retain the tense of the original sentence.

1. The chauffeur is backing up the limousine.

   _____

2. Brian will ask out the French girl.

   _____

3. The judge had written off my statement.

   _____

4. The manager has turned down their offer.

   _____

5. He wrote off his old friend as hopeless.

   _____

Modals

Just as modals can act as auxiliaries to other verbs, so, too, can they act as auxiliaries to phrasal verbs. For example:

You **shouldn't** give up on him so easily.
I **can't** put up with your behavior any longer.
We **ought to** set out on the hike by dawn.

Exercise 97

Rewrite each sentence with the modals provided in parentheses.

1. I was in by midnight. (should, should have, have to)

_____

_____

_____

2. She tries to warm up to him. (must, can, need to)

_____

_____

_____

3. You head for the coast by noon. (should, ought to, want to)

_____

_____

_____

4. Does he throw up in the car? (need to, have to, could have)

_____

_____

_____

5. She doesn't always put up with him. (could, like to, may)

_____

_____

_____

6. Mary is out for the day. (might, be supposed to, must have)

_____

_____

_____

7. Bill doesn't let on about his new job. (should, must, can)

_____

_____

_____

8. Where do they drop off their laundry? (should, have to, should have)

_____

_____

_____

9. The driver backs up here. (can, could have, want to)

_____

_____

_____

10. The clerk takes down the man's testimony. (need to, ought to have, could)

_____

_____

_____

Adverb Position

In certain phrasal verbs, the position of a preposition used as an adverb is not static. For example, the phrase **to work up** means "to prepare or compose." The preposition **up** in that phrase can stand either before or after a noun direct object. But if the direct object is a pronoun, the preposition can only be placed after the pronoun.

> I can work a new report **up** for you. (*noun as direct object*)
> I can work **up** a new report for you. (*noun as direct object*)
> I can work it **up** for you. (*pronoun as direct object*)

Here is another example, with the phrasal verb **to lay off** ("to fire," "to dismiss"):

> The boss laid five people **off**. (*noun as direct object*)
> The boss laid **off** five people. (*noun as direct object*)
> The boss laid them **off**. (*pronoun as direct object*)

Exercise 98

Use the string of elements provided to write two sentences, and place the preposition in each sentence in the two positions possible. Write a third sentence with the direct object noun changed to a direct object pronoun, and place the preposition in the appropriate position.

> I / to fill out / form
> *I fill out the form.*
> *I fill the form out.*
> *I fill it out.*

1. he / to back up / car / into the street

   _____

   _____

2. John / to ask out / pretty girl

   _____

   _____

3. mother / to drop off / children / at school

   _____

   _____

4. to take down / injured man's statement

   _____

   _____

5. little boy / never / to turn down / candy

   _____

   _____

Mastery Check

Exercise 99

With the subject and verb provided, write a present tense phrase that includes a reflexive pronoun. For example:

he / hurt *he hurts himself*

1. she / burn _____
2. I / enjoy _____
3. they / amuse _____
4. we / perjure _____
5. you (sing.) / push _____
6. it / raise _____
7. he / calm _____
8. the women / fan _____
9. Bill and I / help _____
10. you (pl.) / dress _____

Exercise 100

Rewrite each infinitive with the subject provided in parentheses in the two forms of the present tense passive voice. For example:

(it) to start *it is started*
it is being started

1. (it) to steal

_____

_____

2. (she) to kiss

_____

_____

3. (I) to punish

_____

_____

4. (the engineer) to hire

_____

_____

5. (they) to break

_____

_____

6. (you) to invite

_____

_____

7. (the words) to spell

_____

_____

8. (the men) to warn

_____

_____

9. (she) to reward

_____

_____

10. (the boy) to punish

_____

_____

11. (the new hotels) to build

_____

_____

12. (trees) to grow

_____

_____

13. (no one) to suspect

_____

_____

14. (who) to take

_____

_____

15. (something) to lose

_____

_____

Exercise 101

Rewrite each present tense passive sentence in the tenses shown.

1. My wallet is stolen by a pickpocket.

Past: _____

Present perfect: _____

Past perfect: _____

Future: _____

2. Who is accused of the crime?

Past: _____

Present perfect: _____

Past perfect: _____

Future: _____

3. He is being chased by a skunk.

Past: _____

Present perfect: _____

Past perfect: _____

Future: _____

4. The mirror is smashed with a hammer.

Past: _____

Present perfect: _____

Past perfect: _____

Future: _____

5. They are praised by their teacher.

Past: _____

Present perfect: _____

Past perfect: _____

Future: _____

Exercise 102

In the blank provided, write the letter *P* if the past participle in the sentence is in the passive voice. Write the letter *S* if the past participle is in the stative passive.

_____ 1. Is the bedroom painted?

_____ 2. The windows are being washed today.

_____ 3. The children were not allowed to play in the alley.

_____ 4. She is being fired today.

_____ 5. The flower garden is finally planted.

Exercise 103

Rewrite each sentence with the three modal auxiliaries provided in parentheses.

1. It cannot be done. (should, be to, must)

_____

_____

2. The floor needs to be mopped. (be supposed to, ought to have, have to)

_____

_____

_____

Exercise 104

Write the present and past subjunctive forms of the verbs in parentheses to agree with the subjects provided.

1. (to help) we _____ _____
2. (to see) I _____ _____
3. (to make) she _____ _____
4. (to go) it _____ _____
5. (to need) Mary _____ _____
6. (to be) she _____ _____
7. (to warn) they _____ _____
8. (to spend) the girls _____ _____
9. (to eat) he _____ _____
10. (to laugh) you _____ _____
11. (to have) he _____ _____
12. (to drink) I _____ _____
13. (to cut) he _____ _____
14. (to be) I _____ _____
15. (to grow) we _____ _____

Exercise 105

Fill in the blank with the appropriate subjunctive form of the verb provided in parentheses.

1. Tom acts as if the car _____ to him. (to belong)
2. She acted as if I _____ a stranger. (to be)
3. I wish I _____ more money. (to have)
4. If only they _____ spend the day here in the city. (can)
5. He was smiling as if he _____ the answer. (to know)
6. His parents wish he _____ harder last year. (to study)
7. If our daughter just _____ fewer hours. (to work)
8. Suppose it suddenly_____ to snow. (to start)
9. If that _____ only true. (to be)
10. He always wished he _____ in the country as a child. (to live)

Exercise 106

Rewrite the sentences provided with the auxiliaries in parentheses. Change the action to mean an action that is a possibility, a desired outcome, or imaginary. For example:

> She speaks with John. (should)
> *She should have spoken with John.*

1. He reads the small print. (could, ought to, must)

_____

_____

_____

2. I am living in luxury. (could, might, should)

_____

_____

3. My sister fixes the radio. (might, must, should)

_____

_____

4. The girl memorizes Lincoln's Gettysburg Address. (could, must, should)

_____

_____

5. We don't sell our car. (ought to, must, should)

_____

_____

_____

Exercise 107

Look at each sentence. If the word in bold is used as a preposition, write the letter *P* in the blank. If it is used as an adverb, write the letter *A* in the blank.

_____ 1. He wrote **with** a piece of chalk.

_____ 2. Bill came **up** to the woman.

_____ 3. I should send **out** for some burgers.

_____ 4. Zip **up** your jacket.

_____ 5. We never got a postcard **from** them.

_____ 6. You could come **down** with a cold.

_____ 7. No one spoke **out** against the bad law.

_____ 8. My parents were **in** the city.

_____ 9. Jane set **out** on a hike.

_____ 10. He cut an article **out** for me.

Exercise 108

Rewrite each sentence with the modals provided in parentheses.

1. Their son was in by suppertime. (should, should have, have to)

_____

_____

_____

2. We try to warm up to the angry man. (must, can, need to)

_____

_____

_____

3. He heads for the locker room. (should, ought to, want to)

_____

_____

_____

Appendix

Irregular Verbs

Base Form	Simple Past Tense	Past Participle
awake	awoke	awoken
be	was / were	been
bear	bore	born
beat	beat	beat
become	became	become
begin	began	begun
bend	bent	bent
beset	beset	beset
bet	bet	bet
bid	bid / bade	bid / bidden
bind	bound	bound
bite	bit	bitten
bleed	bled	bled
blow	blew	blown
break	broke	broken
breed	bred	bred
bring	brought	brought
broadcast	broadcast	broadcast
build	built	built
burn	burned / burnt	burned / burnt
burst	burst	burst
buy	bought	bought
cast	cast	cast
catch	caught	caught
choose	chose	chosen
cling	clung	clung
come	came	come
cost	cost	cost
creep	crept	crept
cut	cut	cut
deal	dealt	dealt
dig	dug	dug
dive	dived / dove	dived
do	did	done
draw	drew	drawn
dream	dreamed / dreamt	dreamed / dreamt
drive	drove	driven
drink	drank	drunk
eat	ate	eaten
fall	fell	fallen
feed	fed	fed
feel	felt	felt
fight	fought	fought
find	found	found
fit	fit	fit
flee	fled	fled
fling	flung	flung
fly	flew	flown
forbid	forbade	forbidden
forego	forewent	foregone
forget	forgot	forgotten
forgive	forgave	forgiven
forsake	forsook	forsaken
freeze	froze	frozen

Base Form	Simple Past Tense	Past Participle
get	got	gotten
give	gave	given
go	went	gone
grind	ground	ground
grow	grew	grown
hang	hung	hung
hear	heard	heard
hide	hid	hidden
hit	hit	hit
hold	held	held
hurt	hurt	hurt
keep	kept	kept
kneel	knelt	knelt
knit	knit	knit
know	knew	known
lay	laid	laid
lead	led	led
leap	leaped / leapt	leaped / leapt
learn	learned / learnt	learned / learnt
leave	left	left
lend	lent	lent
let	let	let
lie	lay	lain
light	lighted / lit	lighted / lit
lose	lost	lost
make	made	made
mean	meant	meant
meet	met	met
misspell	misspelled / misspelt	misspelled / misspelt
mistake	mistook	mistaken
mow	mowed	mowed / mown
overcome	overcame	overcome
overdo	overdid	overdone
overtake	overtook	overtaken
overthrow	overthrew	overthrown
pay	paid	paid
plead	pled	pled
prove	proved	proved / proven
put	put	put
quit	quit	quit
read	read	read
rid	rid	rid
ride	rode	ridden
ring	rang	rung
rise	rose	risen
run	ran	run
saw	sawed	sawed / sawn
say	said	said
see	saw	seen
seek	sought	sought
sell	sold	sold
send	sent	sent
set	set	set
sew	sewed	sewed / sewn
shake	shook	shaken
shave	shaved	shaved / shaven
shear	sheared	sheared / shorn
shed	shed	shed
shine	shone	shone
shoe	shoed	shoed / shod
shoot	shot	shot
show	showed	shown
shrink	shrank	shrunk
shut	shut	shut

Base Form	Simple Past Tense	Past Participle
sing	sang	sung
sink	sank	sunk
sit	sat	sat
sleep	slept	slept
slay	slew	slain
slide	slid	slid
sling	slung	slung
slit	slit	slit
smite	smote	smitten
sow	sowed	sowed / sown
speak	spoke	spoken
speed	sped	sped
spend	spent	spent
spill	spilled / spilt	spilled / spilt
spin	spun	spun
spit	spit / spat	spit / spat
split	split	split
spread	spread	spread
spring	sprang / sprung	sprung
stand	stood	stood
steal	stole	stolen
stick	stuck	stuck
sting	stung	stung
stink	stank	stunk
stride	strode	stridden
strike	struck	struck
string	strung	strung
strive	strove	striven
swear	swore	sworn
sweep	swept	swept
swell	swelled	swelled / swollen
swim	swam	swum
swing	swung	swung
take	took	taken
teach	taught	taught
tear	tore	torn
tell	told	told
think	thought	thought
throw	threw	thrown
thrust	thrust	thrust
tread	trod	trodden
understand	understood	understood
uphold	upheld	upheld
upset	upset	upset
wake	woke	woken
wear	wore	worn
weave	weaved / wove	weaved / woven
wed	wed	wed
weep	wept	wept
win	won	won
wind	wound	wound
withhold	withheld	withheld
withstand	withstood	withstood
wring	wrung	wrung
write	wrote	written

Answer Key

Exercise 1

1. speak 2. listen 3. forgets 4. worries 5. cries 6. answer 7. surprise 8. buries 9. spend 10. becomes 11. sign, leave 12. likes, lends 13. arranges, pays 14. suggest, allow 15. catches, kisses

Exercise 2

1. are 2. is 3. are 4. am 5. is 6. are 7. are 8. is 9. is 10. are 11. have 12. have 13. has 14. has 15. have 16. have 17. has 18. have 19. has 20. has

Exercise 3

1. borrows, My cousin borrowed my lawn mower. 2. visit, We usually visited our relatives at holiday time. 3. pays, She paid for dinner with a personal check. 4. treat, I treated the boys and girls to some ice cream. 5. follows, He never followed my instructions. 6. calls, Mr. Jennings called a meeting for 5 P.M. 7. tries, No one tried my sister's chocolate cake. 8. say, Rick and Bill said that they want to be astronauts. 9. plan, They planned to take a trip to South America. 10. develops, It developed into a complicated problem.

Exercise 4

Sample answers are provided.
1. He hits the target. He hit the target. 2. It bursts into flames. It burst into flames. 3. I cut a picture out of the newspaper. I cut a picture out of the newspaper. 4. Mark fits into his old jeans. Mark fit into his old jeans. 5. We beat the best team. We beat the best team. 6. She rids us of the problem. She rid us of the problem. 7. Ms. Lopez sets the table for dinner. Ms. Lopez set the table for dinner. 8. You put your coat on the chair. You put your coat on the chair. 9. They wed in the morning. They wed in the morning. 10. My brother-in-law quits his job. My brother-in-law quit his job.

Exercise 5

1. shows, showed 2. gives, gave 3. rids, rid 4. belongs, belonged 5. runs, ran 6. makes, made 7. sends, sent 8. knows, knew 9. tells, told 10. explains, explained 11. waits, waited 12. pleases, pleased 13. brings, brought 14. annoys, annoyed 15. passes, passed 16. wins, won 17. goes, went 18. falls, fell 19. costs, cost 20. rides, rode 21. drinks, drank 22. eats, ate 23. beats, beat 24. creeps, crept 25. meets, met

Exercise 6

1. Martin spoke with his new professor. 2. I was in a very important meeting. 3. My wife bought a new dress or skirt every month. 4. No one understood his dialect. 5. The lawyers had several contracts to discuss. 6. The poor woman screamed in pain. 7. The train left at exactly 10 P.M. 8. You were one of the strongest athletes in the school. 9. They built bridges and tunnels. 10. Someone took them for a drive in the country. 11. Their son grew another inch or two. 12. She had a basket full of colored eggs. 13. We slept until 9:30 A.M. 14. The butcher weighed the three filets of fish. 15. Mr. Jackson told another funny story.

Exercise 7

Sample answers are provided.
1. Bill wanted to spend more time with the children. 2. No one remembers to wish her a happy birthday. 3. I tried to understand the complicated formula. 4. Uncle James forgot to water the lawn. 5. Tina attempts to walk along the edge of the roof.

Exercise 8

1. He will play the piano. He shall play the piano. 2. I shall study English. I will study English. 3. We shall buy a new house. We will buy a new house. 4. She will love the book. She shall love the book. 5. Mark will make no mistakes. Mark shall make no mistakes. 6. The boys will help them. The boys shall help them. 7. No one will be there. No one shall be there. 8. You will eat enough. You shall eat enough. 9. It will need work. It

shall need work. 10. They will practice daily. They shall practice daily. 11. Tina will receive the money. Tina shall receive the money. 12. I shall repair the radio. I will repair the radio. 13. The woman will kiss him. The woman shall kiss him. 14. We shall drive slowly. We will drive slowly. 15. You will stand up. You shall stand up. 16. She will say nothing. She shall say nothing. 17. Everyone will give ten dollars. Everyone shall give ten dollars. 18. Bill and I shall spend less money. Bill and I will spend less money. 19. It will break down. It shall break down. 20. He will pretend. He shall pretend.

Exercise 9

1. she will eat 2. I will look 3. no one will understand 4. Mr. Wills will find 5. we will speak 6. Jim and I will go 7. she will hear 8. they will jump 9. Ms. Garcia will cut 10. you will be 11. the men will drink 12. it will seem 13. something will happen 14. nothing will stop 15. he will see 16. you will buy 17. I will think 18. we will hurry 19. the child will cry 20. it will have

Exercise 10

1. Will he spend a lot of money? 2. Will they hurry home? 3. Shall I buy this blouse? 4. Will Donald study here? 5. Will Bill be in Europe? 6. Shall we help them? 7. Will my cousins live in New York? 8. Will you lose your wallet again? 9. Will she fall down? 10. Will it smell good? 11. Shall the boys and I (*or* Shall we) play checkers? 12. Will you spell it correctly? 13. Will a woman become president? 14. Will someone forget this book? 15. Shall I be your partner? 16. Shall you and I (*or* Shall we) work together? 17. Will my answer be right? 18. Will they swim to shore? 19. Will her questions be difficult? 20. Shall we play in a band? 21. Will Sarah become a doctor? 22. Will he sing in the choir? 23. Will the plant grow fast? 24. Will someone help me? 25. Will that hurt?

Exercise 11

1. I have found 2. they have begun 3. Mark has thought 4. she has studied 5. we have arranged 6. it has broken 7. you have pretended 8. he has been 9. Ms. Brown has forgotten 10. each boy has tried 11. Tom and I have danced 12. the woman has knit 13. someone has shouted 14. I have known 15. you have come 16. it has rained 17. no one has remembered 18. we have lent 19. someone has knocked 20. it has bled 21. you have had 22. they have been 23. Maria has allowed 24. we have spent 25. it has cost

Exercise 12

1. we had become 2. I had cried 3. you had followed 4. someone had hit 5. they had called 6. the boys had played 7. she had sung 8. it had rung 9. the clouds had moved 10. I had driven 11. the girls and I had laughed 12. it had stormed 13. he had married 14. John had wed 15. we had flown

Exercise 13

1. my landlady will have said 2. you will have bargained 3. they will have traveled 4. she will have spent 5. someone will have reminded 6. it will have been 7. Martin will have had 8. I will have belonged 9. we will have sold 10. life will have been 11. my daughter will have become 12. it will have ended 13. they will have died 14. an explorer will have climbed 15. he will have known

Exercise 14

Sample answers are provided.
1. bring some snacks 2. invite Ms. Brown 3. explain this already 4. break into our house 5. get home by noon 6. get a little better 7. rent the apartment 8. visit Colorado 9. write a new contract 10. meet your goals 11. take care of your children 12. make a campfire by the weekend 13. have next Monday off 14. join the army 15. complete the job by tomorrow

Exercise 15

Sample answers are provided.
1. pretty 2. lucky 3. surprised 4. unhappy 5. rainy 6. together 7. satisfied 8. the first chairman 9. good friends 10. a star 11. an athlete 12. foreign tourists 13. the happiest children 14. me 15. you

Exercise 16

Sample answers are provided.

1. sweet 2. angry 3. nervous 4. welcome 5. faint 6. strange 7. so bad 8. wrong 9. fantastic 10. happy

Exercise 17

Sample answers are provided.

1. This will become serious for them. This will become a serious problem for them. 2. Mary became frustrated. Mary became a nurse. 3. My father wanted to remain healthy. My father wanted to remain a security guard. 4. She remained upset. She remained a teacher.

Exercise 18

1. L 2. L 3. T 4. L 5. L 6. L 7. T 8. L 9. T 10. L 11. L 12. L 13. L 14. L 15. L 16. T 17. L 18. L 19. L 20. L

Exercise 19

1. T 2. T 3. I 4. T 5. I 6. I 7. T 8. I 9. I 10. I 11. I 12. T 13. I 14. T 15. I 16. T 17. T 18. I 19. I 20. I 21. T 22. I 23. I 24. T 25. I

Exercise 20

1. She is supposed to stay with her mother. She needs to stay with her mother. She wishes to stay with her mother. 2. They want to perform in a circus. They used to perform in a circus. They have got to perform in a circus. 3. You have to memorize the poem. You are to memorize the poem. You ought to memorize the poem. 4. We like to relax in the garden. We are allowed to relax in the garden. We need to relax in the garden. 5. Jim wishes to be a good cook. Jim wants to be a good cook. Jim is supposed to be a good cook.

Exercise 21

1. *Past*: I was supposed to play. *Present perfect*: X. *Future*: X. 2. *Past*: She wanted to learn. *Present perfect*: She has wanted to learn. *Future*: She will want to learn. 3. *Past*: They ought to have hurried. *Present perfect*: X. *Future*: X. 4. *Past*: No one liked to eat it. *Present perfect*: No has liked to eat it. *Future*: No one will like to eat it. 5. *Past*: We were allowed to listen. *Present perfect*: We have been allowed to listen. *Future*: We will be allowed to listen. 6. *Past*: Betty needed to rest. *Present perfect*: Betty has needed to rest. *Future*: Betty will need to rest. 7. *Past*: Someone had to help. *Present perfect*: Someone has had to help. *Future*: Someone will have to help. 8. *Past*: X. *Present perfect*: X. *Future*: X. 9. *Past*: You were to help them. *Present perfect*: X. *Future*: X. 10. *Past*: X. *Present perfect*: X. *Future*: X.

Exercise 22

1. The team must hurry to the stadium. 2. Someone can unlock the door for you. 3. Tim had better study hard for his final exams. 4. I would learn as much as I can about her. 5. This may be a good way to get to know one another. 6. Charles might come along when we visit Graceland. 7. Everyone should use good manners. 8. Erik could have spoken with his angry neighbors. 9. Your son had better have had the money for the payment. 10. Perhaps she may have needed some help. 11. Someone might have seen the accident happen. 12. They must have gone to the movies. 13. You should have gotten more sleep. 14. I would have planned a party for you. 15. My friends better vote in the election.

Exercise 23

1. The students are to report to the auditorium. 2. My parents have to spend a lot of time in the country. 3. Mark ought to have asked a better question. 4. The boys must have fallen asleep. 5. This might be the right thing to do. 6. They could see a house in the distance. 7. No one is allowed to touch his stamp collection. 8. This should be a good lesson for you. 9. I should have listened to my father. 10. Mr. Bennett can speak three languages. 11. She may have forgotten my name. 12. The girls had to leave the meeting early. 13. I have sometimes needed to nap after work. 14. They ought to hold down their voices. 15. Dad likes to play games with the children. 16. The Johnsons used to live across the street from us. 17. I could see the anger in his

eyes. 18. He was supposed to wash the dishes every day. 19. Maria will have to return to Miami. 20. We have always wanted to travel to Korea. 21. The hikers were to take the path on the right. 22. You had better have a good excuse. 23. She wished to become a ballerina. 24. The neighbors upstairs have got to stop the noise. 25. My brother will have to take the bus to work.

Exercise 24

Sample answers are provided.
1. Mr. Kelly always fixed the old car. 2. I borrowed ten dollars from her every payday. 3. We were never interested in his poems. 4. My grandfather often had a serious illness. 5. Each day regularly became longer and longer. 6. It occasionally smelled awful in his room. 7. John went to school with his little sister every Monday. 8. The twins always liked turkey sandwiches. 9. My uncle frequently made a large salad for supper. 10. They traveled to Asia twice a year. 11. I always spend my last dollar. 12. Andrea danced with the young man from France two times. 13. We sometimes began the lesson from Chapter 2. 14. The girls were occasionally late to soccer practice. 15. You never spoke in German with her. 16. The sheets rarely felt damp. 17. Everyone always had a good time at my party. 18. My neighbor came by for a visit all the time. 19. Barbara sometimes took the children for a walk. 20. Tim and I often lived off the land.

Exercise 25

1. C; My cousin has broken the vase. My cousin will break the vase. 2. H; We have never played chess. We will never play chess. 3. H; I have usually written my letters in pencil. I will usually write my letters in pencil. 4. C; There has been a loud noise in the hall. There will be a loud noise in the hall. 5. C; Someone has knocked at the door. Someone will knock at the door. 6. C; Laura has wanted a diamond ring. Laura will want a diamond ring. 7. H; Most of the time, she has worked in a drugstore. Most of the time, she will work in a drugstore. 8. H; My son has visited me once a year. My son will visit me once a year. 9. H; The men have frequently stopped for a cool drink. The men will frequently stop for a cool drink. 10. H; I have continually asked for your help. I will continually ask for your help. 11. H; She has rarely risked her money on a bet. She will rarely risk her money on a bet. 12. C; Donald has fainted. Donald will faint. 13. H; We have watered the lawn every day. We will water the lawn every day. 14. H; The boys have hardly ever helped us. The boys will hardly ever help us. 15. C; I have been in Chicago for a week. I will be in Chicago for a week.

Exercise 26

1. I 2. C 3. C 4. I 5. I 6. C 7. I 8. I 9. C 10. I

Exercise 27

1. we are studying 2. she has been learning 3. no one is speaking 4. I had been taking 5. you are being 6. it is becoming 7. they will be arguing 8. Mark is being 9. he was drinking 10. I am writing 11. it was starting 12. you have been following 13. time is going 14. we were sharing 15. I will be dressing 16. she will have been swimming 17. the children were being 18. we have been going 19. Tina was being 20. he was spending

Exercise 28

1. playing, arrived 2. been 3. relaxing, started 4. am / was 5. arrived, was 6. sitting, reading 7. began, were 8. be, come 9. have 10. pretending 11. writing, burst 12. be, begins 13. is / was 14. was 15. been

Exercise 29

1. Were we (Were you) in Germany last summer? 2. Is she giving a speech in San Diego? 3. Am I (Are you) certain that I am (you are) right? 4. Was someone tampering with the lock? 5. Is my (your) nephew serving in the Air Force? 6. Was Mr. Kelly shoveling snow in the driveway? 7. Are these pants too tight? 8. Were you (Was I) being very stubborn again? 9. Am I (Are you) thinking of staying another week in Denver? 10. Was it difficult to understand? 11. Was it storming the night he was born? 12. Is she my (your) wife and my (your) best friend? 13. Were they the first of our (your) friends to become citizens? 14. Is it finally getting warm again? 15. Was John dancing with Bill's wife?

Exercise 30

1. Did Daniel break the expensive, new mirror? 2. Did I (you) sell the little house on the lake? 3. Does Martin bring her flowers every week? 4. Does she love his latest novel? 5. Were we (Were you) swimming in Lake Michigan? 6. Did Ms. Garcia buy a cottage in the mountains? 7. Does somebody know the correct answer? 8. Is Havana the capital city of Cuba? 9. Does Jim really speak four languages? 10. Did Ben have a problem with his car again? 11. Did you fill out the form incorrectly? 12. Does her brother have her car today? 13. Were the little boys playing with the new pups? 14. Did the doctor place a cast on his broken ankle? 15. Do they stand on the corner and chat for a long time? 16. Am I (Are you) sick of these arguments? 17. Did she learn of Tom's illness today? 18. Is the river warm enough for swimming? 19. Does Mark build a cabinet for his girlfriend? 20. Did he land the little plane in a field?

Exercise 31

1. Had Mr. Roberts lived in Asia all his life? 2. Will the girls help repair the chairs? 3. Have I (you) become quite ill again? 4. Will Tina prepare some lunch for us? 5. Had you already seen that movie? 6. Has someone taken my glasses from my desk? 7. Will they arrive here by 10 P.M.? 8. Will it be late when Mark gets home? 9. Has Aunt Mary gone to her country home? 10. Had Bill always liked your cooking?

Exercise 32

1. Shall, 1 2. Shall, 1 3. Will, 2 4. Shall, 1 5. Will, 2 6. Shall, 1 7. Will, 2 8. Will, 2 9. Shall, 1 10. Will, 2

Exercise 33

1. Did we have to live? 2. Will he be allowed to sing? 3. Does she like to write? 4. Were you to arrive? 5. Was someone supposed to buy? 6. Must I think? 7. Did we used to argue? 8. Ought you to speak? 9. Will they wish to test? 10. Had he needed to stay?

Exercise 34

1. Who has taken a trip to China? 2. Which tie looks better on me (you)? 3. How far are the German tourists traveling? 4. Why did she cry so hard? 5. How often do we (you) work out? 6. What made a profit for them every year? 7. What did he find in an old chest? 8. Whose wife is a Hollywood actress? 9. When can you bring those boxes to me? 10. What was stolen from the museum?

Exercise 35

1. Come home early. 2. Stay home from work. 3. Listen to these new CDs. 4. Sing in a choir. 5. Borrow a lawn mower from the neighbors. 6. Water the vegetable garden and the flowers. 7. Believe me. 8. Be quiet. 9. Go to the movies with friends. 10. Have a hamburger with fries. 11. Turn on the lights. 12. Return the books tomorrow. 13. Stand up. 14. Sleep in that large tent. 15. Run to the store. 16. Kiss the children good-night. 17. Be smart about this. 18. Hurry to the hospital. 19. Look into the mirror and be surprised. 20. Sit down and take your shoes off.

Exercise 36

1. Let's take a drive out to Lake Tahoe. 2. Let's try to be fair about this. 3. Let's test the soil for insects. 4. Let's not bother the newborn kittens. 5. Let's write Karen a couple postcards. 6. Let's be on time more often. 7. Let's spend a lot more time talking. 8. Let's forget about the problems with the car. 9. Let's arrange for a taxi. 10. Let's get home before sunset. 11. Let's earn some extra money. 12. Let's go out dancing. 13. Let's donate some money to their cause. 14. Let's join an athletic club. 15. Let's be more helpful. 16. Let's practice kicking goals. 17. Let's plan our winter vacation. 18. Let's take the bus to town. 19. Let's bathe that smelly dog. 20. Let's rent an apartment in the city.

Exercise 37

1. Let the soldiers stop under a shady tree. 2. Don't let my father give them more money. 3. Let me recommend a good restaurant to you. 4. Let her ask for a raise. 5. Let the lawyers agree on the selling price. 6. Let Mark explain it to you. 7. Don't let some other person work on this job. 8. Let them make a list of their

complaints. 9. Let him pretend he doesn't know us. 10. Let it happen naturally. 11. Let the balloons float into the sky. 12. Let him be captain of the team. 13. Let her husband do it for her. 14. Let me change my clothes. 15. Let that be a warning to you. 16. Let the dogs sleep in the garage. 17. Let them wear some funny costumes. 18. Let Anna help with the puzzle. 19. Let me answer. 20. Let your friend lend you the money.

Exercise 38

1. 1 or 4 2. 1 3. 2 4. 1 5. 1 6. 1 or 4 7. 3 8. 1 or 4 9. 4 10. 1 11. 3 12. 2 13. 1 14. 1 15. 4 16. 2 17. 1 18. 3 19. 1 20. 1

Exercise 39

1. Mike did not speak with the landlord. 2. I did not hold open the door. 3. We will not arrive on time. 4. Lightning does not strike the tree. 5. Will your father not help us? 6. Jim will not travel by train. 7. I do not like hiking in the rain. 8. Mary has not broken her arm. 9. Had they not lived here long? 10. You should not buy a house in town. 11. Our vacation did not go by too fast. 12. He has not kept the money for himself. 13. You do not write very well. 14. The children have not been learning French. 15. Your voice does not sound angry. 16. I did not see them at the store. 17. What did you not sell? 18. Shall I not serve dinner? 19. They do not come from Cuba. 20. Jean did not send her a postcard.

Exercise 40

1. She does not see anyone. 2. Has he not found anything? 3. They are not going anywhere. 4. Tom does not hurt anybody. 5. We did not lose any time. 6. I do not believe anyone. 7. This is not anything. 8. They did not get anywhere. 9. I had not questioned anybody. 10. They will not receive any gifts.

Exercise 41

1. wouldn't 2. mustn't 3. isn't allowed 4. couldn't 5. won't 6. hadn't 7. needn't 8. weren't 9. haven't been 10. won't be 11. doesn't 12. didn't 13. wasn't able to 14. weren't supposed to 15. aren't

Exercise 42

1. they've not 2. we're not 3. it's not 4. I'd not 5. she'll not 6. you've not 7. Sarah's not 8. you'd not 9. he's not 10. they'll not

Exercise 43

1. Laura didn't dance with the landlord. 2. I didn't hold her hand. 3. We won't depart on time. 4. The boys aren't asleep. 5. Can't your father help us? 6. I won't travel by bus. 7. Don't you like playing the guitar? 8. The boy hasn't broken his arm. 9. Hadn't he worked here long? 10. You wouldn't buy a car from him. 11. Can't they go to the store? 12. She hasn't kept the puppy warm. 13. You don't sing very well. 14. They haven't been learning about Mexico. 15. That song doesn't sound sad. 16. He didn't see them yesterday. 17. We didn't buy it from Mr. Garcia. 18. She didn't do it wrong. 19. Dad mustn't try to bake a cake. 20. I shouldn't speak with her.

Exercise 44

Sample answers are provided.
1. I usually spent my money wisely. I have always spent my money wisely. I will rarely spend my money wisely. 2. She often sat with me. She has sometimes sat with me. She will occasionally sit with me. 3. Bob usually wrote me. Bob has never written me. Bob will frequently write me. 4. He rushed home excitedly. He has rushed home in a panic. He will rush home speedily. 5. She spoke the words gently. She has spoken the words harshly. She will speak the words clearly. 6. They turned the corner rapidly. They have turned the corner slowly. They will turn the corner cautiously.

Exercise 45

1. rarely 2. never 3. early 4. with a little grin 5. today 6. on his bike 7. always 8. only once 9. during summer 10. gladly 11. fast 12. often 13. seldom 14. yesterday 15. with a loud bang

Exercise 46

1. P 2. P 3. T 4. T 5. P 6. P 7. P 8. P 9. P 10. P 11. T 12. P 13. T 14. T 15. P

Exercise 47

1. extremely 2. rather 3. really 4. too 5. almost 6. rather 7. quite 8. too 9. perfectly 10. extremely

Exercise 48

1. Who was speaking? Who has been speaking? Who will be speaking? 2. I was going home. I have been going home. I will be going home. 3. Were you helping? Have you been helping? Will you be helping? 4. Marie was crying. Marie has been crying. Marie will be crying. 5. The children were playing. The children have been playing. The children will be playing.

Exercise 49

1. a napping woman / a woman napping 2. the cat chasing a mouse 3. the spinning top / the top spinning 4. a team winning again 5. a developing story / a story developing 6. the reading boys / the boys reading 7. a student studying hard 8. a river running through the valley 9. gently falling snow / snow gently falling 10. music filling my ears 11. something puzzling me 12. the loudly crashing waves / the waves loudly crashing 13. the waves crashing on the beach 14. rain filling the streets 15. slowly blooming flowers / flowers slowly blooming 16. someone yelling a lot 17. a book costing more than twenty dollars 18. the rather boring class 19. people exaggerating everything 20. storms destroying homes

Exercise 50

1. spelled 2. written 3. sold 4. happened 5. seen 6. said 7. fit 8. watched 9. pleased 10. found 11. helped 12. controlled 13. developed 14. sent 15. made 16. shown 17. brought 18. known 19. thought 20. been

Exercise 51

1. Who had spoken? Who will have spoken? 2. I had taught. I will have taught. 3. She had been. She will have been. 4. You had broken. You will have broken. 5. We had slept. We will have slept.

Exercise 52

1. the apple eaten by Jack 2. the written word / the word written 3. arrested people / people arrested 4. a girl kissed by him 5. a church built in the city / a church being built in the city 6. music heard throughout the house 7. a room painted red 8. the repaired car / the car repaired / the car being repaired 9. the barn set on fire 10. the much photographed movie star / the movie star much photographed / the movie star photographed much 11. the bedroom richly decorated / the bedroom decorated richly / the richly decorated bedroom 12. the child gently placed on the bed 13. the successfully completed operation / the operation successfully completed / the operation completed successfully / the operation being successfully completed / the operation being completed successfully 14. a car buried by the snow 15. carelessly burned leaves / leaves carelessly burned / leaves burned carelessly 16. just polished shoes / shoes just polished 17. candy eaten / candy being eaten 18. a village reached only by air 19. the stopped vehicles / the vehicles stopped 20. slowly developed film / film slowly developed / film developed slowly

Exercise 53

1. D 2. D 3. AV 4. C 5. S 6. S 7. AV 8. AJ 9. AJ 10. S

Exercise 54

1. a. them to hurry home b. you to help wash the car c. someone to find a solution d. her to dance with me e. Bill to fix the bicycle 2. a. me to lend him ten dollars b. us to drive him home c. him to come for dinner d. the girls to meet him in an hour e. no one to join him 3. a. her to return by noon b. them to eat a good lunch c. Tom to set his alarm clock d. you to buy some milk e. Mark and Sue to stay in their rooms 4. a. us

to sort the mail b. her to type some letters c. me to work in the warehouse d. the men to repair the furnace e. him to clean the office

Exercise 55

1. a. them to come here every day b. to receive a good salary 2. a. me to pay you a visit b. to use my laptop 3. a. her to apply for the job b. to introduce them to our son 4. a. anyone to use my credit card b. to stay here very long

Exercise 56

1. P 2. S 3. C 4. P 5. P 6. S 7. C 8. S 9. P 10. D 11. D 12. S 13. P 14. D 15. C

Exercise 57

1. a. your complaining about the food b. snoring at night 2. a. her being so courageous b. trying to give up smoking 3. a. his (John's) joking about such things b. strolling through the park 4. a. their gossiping about me b. working in such humidity 5. a. our visiting on another day b. traveling to South America 6. a. his acting in that play b. spending time with you 7. a. her (Mary's) punishing the boys so much b. drinking the stale tea 8. a. your cooking any day b. remaining here for the week 9. a. my chatting with Jim b. wearing your new suit 10. a. her being promoted b. winning the lottery

Exercise 58

1. has, her 2. lowers, his / her 3. hears, his 4. Its, is 5. his, is 6. can, its 7. provides, his 8. has, his / her 9. left, her 10. handed, his / her

Exercise 59

Sample answers are provided.
1. wants to sell his / her car 2. owns his / her own house 3. has his / her ticket ready 4. has lost his / her wallet 5. has his / her own car

Exercise 60

1. is 2. is 3. They 4. their 5. it 6. is 7. doesn't 8. its 9. its 10. is

Exercise 61

1. has / have 2. is 3. ought to 4. forms 5. is 6. makes 7. carries 8. becomes 9. must 10. needs

Exercise 62

1. is 2. is 3. is 4. is / are 5. is 6. is 7. are 8. is 9. is 10. are 11. has 12. have 13. have 14. has 15. has 16. has 17. has 18. has 19. have 20. has 21. does 22. does 23. does 24. do 25. does 26. does 27. does 28. do 29. does 30. do

Exercise 63

1. are 2. wasn't 3. Are 4. are 5. ought to be 6. was 7. were 8. is 9. will be 10. must be

Exercise 64

1. yet, of course, she had some problems; yet, of course, she has had some problems; yet, of course, she had had some problems; yet, of course, she will have some problems 2. The room got cold; The room has gotten cold; The room had gotten cold; The room will get cold 3. for the temperature was changing; for the temperature has been changing; for the temperature had been changing; for the temperature will be changing 4. but the weather was turning cold; but the weather has been turning cold; but the weather had been turning cold; but the weather will be turning cold 5. and was looking for work; and has been looking for work; and had been looking for work; and will be looking for work 6. but the golf tournament was on Friday; but the golf tournament will be on Friday 7. nor will I approve of it 8. have you seen that film; had you seen that film

Exercise 65

1. are 2. is 3. are 4. is 5. is 6. are 7. are 8. is 9. are 10. is 11. are 12. are 13. is 14. is 15. is

Exercise 66

1. stay 2. will lock 3. will have to 4. had been working 5. arrived 6. prepare 7. will see 8. can / will 9. met 10. want

Exercise 67

1. don't visit 2. are 3. felt 4. is 5. was 6. see 7. have to 8. were 9. will go 10. is

Exercise 68

1. is turning 2. will build 3. will bring 4. is 5. hates 6. am going 7. will lose 8. will live 9. is / was / will be 10. loves 11. won't work 12. knows 13. is 14. want to 15. gets 16. is 17. ask 18. was 19. understand 20. joins

Exercise 69

1. angry 2. another letter 3. washed 4. rather hot 5. your new car 6. home 7. my hair trimmed 8. the TV repaired 9. you 10. to the hotel 11. a strange package 12. my boss 13. an answer 14. happy 15. a new passport 16. these documents filed 17. to Toronto 18. a note from her 19. her 20. to your room

Exercise 70

1. E 2. A 3. C 4. F 5. D 6. B 7. B 8. A 9. D 10. E 11. F 12. E 13. D 14. A 15. A 16. C 17. A 18. E 19. F 20. B

Exercise 71

1. I get the meaning across to them. I got the meaning across to them. I have gotten the meaning across to them. I will get the meaning across to them. 2. They never get ahead. They never got ahead. They have never gotten ahead. They will never get ahead. 3. The boys get along well. The boys got along well. The boys have gotten along well. The boys will get along well. 4. She gets at the source of the problem. She got at the source of the problem. She has gotten at the source of the problem. She will get at the source of the problem. 5. Who gets away with a crime? Who got away with a crime? Who has gotten away with a crime? Who will get away with a crime?

Exercise 72

1. prosper 2. become 3. understand 4. have the opportunity 5. emphatic must 6. arrive 7. furnish 8. wake up 9. cooperate 10. provoke someone to act 11. go 12. emphatic have 13. meet 14. receive 15. succeed with little effort 16. recover 17. hint 18. provoke someone to act 19. have something done 20. become

Exercise 73

1. means 2. causes 3. is 4. shocks 5. makes 6. sank 7. has to be 8. horrifies 9. are 10. brings 11. was 12. are made / were made 13. are / were 14. causes 15. brings

Exercise 74

1. respect 2. likes 3. are 4. hasn't 5. was 6. has 7. am 8. are 9. were 10. had baked 11. frightened 12. are receiving 13. are 14. gets 15. was

Exercise 75

1. where 2. where 3. when 4. why 5. where 6. why 7. where 8. when 9. why 10. when 11. when 12. where 13. why 14. when 15. where

Exercise 76

1. that you needed to meet; that you have needed to meet; that you had needed to meet; that you will need to meet 2. that were in relatively good shape; that have been in relatively good shape; that had been in relatively good shape 3. who was the chairman of the committee; who has been the chairman of the committee; who had been the chairman of the committee; who will be the chairman of the committee 4. which frightened me to death; which has frightened me to death; which had frightened me to death 5. whose uncle lived in Mexico; whose uncle has lived in Mexico; whose uncle had lived in Mexico; whose uncle will live in Mexico 6. that were dubbed in English; that have been dubbed in English; that had been dubbed in English 7. that eased the pain; that has eased the pain; that had eased the pain; that will ease the pain 8. that took place in Asia; that has taken place in Asia; that had taken place in Asia; that will take place in Asia 9. who worked in this store; who have worked in this store; who had worked in this store; who will work in this store 10. whom you met; whom you have met; whom you had met; whom you will meet 11. which were planted in this park; which have been planted in this park; which had been planted in this park; which will be planted in this park 12. that will need a ride 13. where there was peace and quiet; where there has been peace and quiet; where there had been peace and quiet; where there will be peace and quiet 14. when their car had broken down 15. which made the entire team very proud; which has made the entire team very proud; which had made the entire team very proud

Exercise 77

1. **ourselves** We blamed ourselves for the problem. We have blamed ourselves for the problem. We had blamed ourselves for the problem. We will blame ourselves for the problem. 2. **myself** I behaved myself rather badly. I have behaved myself rather badly. I had behaved myself rather badly. I will behave myself rather badly. 3. **yourselves** You enjoyed yourselves at my party. You have enjoyed yourselves at my party. You had enjoyed yourselves at my party. You will enjoy yourselves at my party. 4. **herself** She didn't control herself. She hasn't controlled herself. She hadn't controlled herself. She won't control herself. 5. **themselves** Were they washing themselves? Have they been washing themselves? Had they been washing themselves? Will they be washing themselves? 6. **ourselves** Mary and I amused ourselves with a game. Mary and I have amused ourselves with a game. Mary and I had amused ourselves with a game. Mary and I will amuse ourselves with a game. 7. **themselves** They prided themselves on their looks. They have prided themselves on their looks. They had prided themselves on their looks. They will pride themselves on their looks. 8. **yourself** You guarded yourself against danger. You have guarded yourself against danger. You had guarded yourself against danger. You will guard yourself against danger. 9. **herself** His mother braced herself against a chair. His mother has braced herself against a chair. His mother had braced herself against a chair. His mother will brace herself against a chair. 10. **myself** I didn't really like myself. I haven't really liked myself. I hadn't really liked myself. I won't really like myself.

Exercise 78

1. John needs some medicine for himself. 2. I do not permit myself to smoke. 3. She buys herself a new dress. 4. They are interested in themselves. 5. The boys behave themselves so well. 6. Why does Mary send herself flowers? 7. You must lend yourselves some money. 8. The professor is thinking to himself. 9. The players are proud of themselves. 10. Why do you blame yourself? 11. The old man gives himself a birthday present. 12. We should not speak of ourselves. 13. You send yourself a reminder. 14. He calls himself a winner. 15. It raises itself off the ground.

Exercise 79

1. My brother and sister repaired the car themselves. 2. We took care of the little children ourselves. 3. I baked a cake myself. 4. She struggled against the current herself. 5. Did you build these toys yourself? 6. The baby crawled across the floor by himself / herself. 7. No one could survive here by himself / herself. 8. Did they carry the heavy timbers by themselves? 9. You stacked the firewood by yourselves. 10. My sister and I carried the suitcases by ourselves. 11. We ourselves drew up a new contract. 12. I myself spent no money on gambling. 13. Jack himself regretted the argument. 14. Could you yourself take responsibility for it? 15. They themselves didn't understand this illness.

Exercise 80

(Either **one another** or **each other** is correct.)

1. You and I care for one another. / We care for one another. 2. The men and the boss joke with one another. 3. The squirrel and the raccoon hide from one another. 4. Bob and Jim don't like one another. 5. The old elk and the young elk challenge one another. 6. We smile at one another. / You and I smile at one another. 7. The women and the men don't see one another. 8. His story and your story contradict one another. 9. Michael and the tourists help one another. 10. We like one another. / He and I like one another.

Exercise 81

1. The keys were lost by her. The keys have been lost by her. The keys had been lost by her. The keys will be lost by her. 2. My car was stolen by a thief. My car has been stolen by a thief. My car had been stolen by a thief. My car will be stolen by a thief. 3. She was being watched by someone. She has been watched by someone. She had been watched by someone. She will be watched by someone. 4. Who was arrested by the police? Who has been arrested by the police? Who had been arrested by the police? Who will be arrested by the police? 5. I was being chased by a bear. I have been chased by a bear. I had been chased by a bear. I will be chased by a bear. 6. The duck was shot by a hunter. The duck has been shot by a hunter. The duck had been shot by a hunter. The duck will be shot by a hunter. 7. The window was smashed by a rock. The window has been smashed by a rock. The window had been smashed by a rock. The window will be smashed by a rock. 8. The candle was blown out by the wind. The candle has been blown out by the wind. The candle had been blown out by the wind. The candle will be blown out by the wind. 9. We were praised by our boss. We have been praised by our boss. We had been praised by our boss. We will be praised by our boss. 10. Was Laura being stopped by the guard? Has Laura been stopped by the guard? Had Laura been stopped by the guard? Will Laura be stopped by the guard?

Exercise 82

1. An oath has been taken by them. 2. The birds are being watched by Mark. 3. Her car is being borrowed by me. 4. A song will be sung by Jean. 5. A bottle of wine had been brought by the men. 6. The engine was being checked by the mechanics. 7. His novel was published by a new company. 8. Was the puppy hurt by him? 9. Several postcards were written by Mary. 10. The bedroom has not been painted by us. 11. This school will be attended by the best students. 12. France was being toured by the American tourists. 13. By whom was the door repaired? 14. Something interesting is found by the professor. 15. The windows are being opened by the landlady. 16. A new couch was purchased by him. 17. The bill was paid by Bill. 18. The new CD had not been heard by them. 19. The kitchen will be cleaned by both of us. 20. The movie was recommended by me.

Exercise 83

1. The girl is sent a bouquet by Mark. A bouquet is sent to the girl by Mark. 2. She has been brought some magazines by us. Some magazines have been brought to her by us. 3. Each of us will be bought a candy bar by Mr. Locke. A candy bar will be bought for each of us by Mr. Locke. 4. I am given an award by the mayor. An award is given to me by the mayor. 5. Mary was shipped the wrong dress by the store. The wrong dress was shipped to Mary by the store.

Exercise 84

1. A rock was thrown at him. 2. His poetry will never be understood. 3. A terrible problem was being caused. 4. Too much time was taken. 5. We had been warned before. 6. A bad scar will be left. 7. The houses have been built close together. 8. The memorial is visited every summer. 9. Will the wheat be planted in this field? 10. My lunch was being eaten.

Exercise 85

1. P 2. P 3. P 4. P 5. S 6. S 7. P 8. P 9. S 10. P 11. S 12. P 13. S 14. P 15. P

Exercise 86

1. we can be persuaded 2. I am allowed to be coached 3. she ought to be taught 4. he had better be punished 5. you must be rewarded 6. they could be fined 7. he has to be guided 8. it needs to be fixed 9. they are supposed to be introduced 10. who wishes to be elected 11. they have got to be reminded 12. I am to be married 13. you may be surrounded 14. that might be undertaken 15. we used to be admired 16. it would be proved 17. she has to be fired 18. they should be presented 19. I wish to be flattered 20. he likes to be kissed

Exercise 87

1. *Past*: I had to be hired for the job. *Present perfect*: I have had to be hired for the job. *Past perfect*: I had had to be hired for the job. *Future*: I will have to be hired for the job. 2. *Past*: You ought to have been fired. *Present perfect*: X. *Past perfect*: X. *Future*: X. 3. *Past*: She wasn't able to be reached by phone. *Present perfect*: She hasn't been able to be reached by phone. *Past perfect*: She hadn't been able to be reached by phone. *Future*: She won't be able to be reached by phone. 4. *Past*: Could it be repaired? *Present perfect*: X. *Past perfect*: X. *Future*: X. 5. *Past*: You were to be commended. *Present perfect*: X. *Past perfect*: X. *Future*: X. 6. *Past*: That needed to be done properly. *Present perfect*: That has needed to be done properly. *Past perfect*: That had needed to be done properly. *Future*: That will need to be done properly. 7. *Past*: The meat was supposed to be roasted. *Present perfect*: X. *Past perfect*: X. *Future*: X. 8. *Past*: The dog didn't like to be bathed. *Present perfect*: The dog hasn't liked to be bathed. *Past perfect*: The dog hadn't liked to be bathed. *Future*: The dog won't like to be bathed. 9. *Past*: She wanted to be dressed as a queen. *Present perfect*: She has wanted to be dressed as a queen. *Past perfect*: She had wanted to be dressed as a queen. *Future*: She will want to be dressed as a queen. 10. *Past*: Her poems might be published. *Present perfect*: X. *Past perfect*: X. *Future*: X.

Exercise 88

1. It should not be done. It is not to be done. It must not be done. 2. The floor is supposed to be mopped. The floor ought to be mopped. The floor had better be mopped. 3. Mr. Peters wished to be paid. Mr. Peters could be paid. Mr. Peters had to be paid. 4. Should you be punished? Would you be punished? Did you need to be punished? 5. Mark isn't supposed to be annoyed by his sister. Mark may not be annoyed by his sister. Mark must not be annoyed by his sister. 6. The problem is able to be solved. The problem needs to be solved. The problem might be solved. 7. It ought to have been lost. It could have been lost. It may have been lost. 8. This document could not be copied. This document is not supposed to be copied. This document ought not to be copied. 9. He used to be complimented for his looks. He wished to be complimented for his looks. He should have been complimented for his looks. 10. It must have been broken by your son. It would be broken by your son. It might be broken by your son.

Exercise 89

1. help, helped 2. see, saw 3. make, made 4. do, did 5. want, wanted 6. be, were 7. warn, warned 8. spend, spent 9. drink, drank 10. laugh, laughed 11. have, had 12. eat, ate 13. grow, grew 14. be, were 15. carry, carried 16. catch, caught 17. allow, allowed 18. be, were 19. cut, cut 20. sing, sang

Exercise 90

1. lives 2. see 3. be 4. push 5. prepare 6. be 7. stop 8. drink 9. help 10. be 11. can 12. solve 13. be 14. return 15. remain 16. sign 17. be 18. worry 19. pay 20. be

Exercise 91

1. belonged 2. were 3. had 4. could 5. knew 6. had studied 7. lived 8. started 9. were 10. had lived 11. were 12. told 13. had met 14. had 15. spoke

Exercise 92

1. If we were in Mexico, we would go shopping every afternoon. 2. If you had a down payment, you could buy this car. 3. If the weather were better, the boys would go hiking. 4. If my family lived in the capital, I would visit the museums every day. 5. If the plane landed early, we could get downtown by 5 P.M. 6. If she

caught a plane, she might be in New York by dusk. 7. If I understood your language, I would be happy to chat with you. 8. If you slept longer, you would have more energy. 9. If the circus came to town, we would go there every day. 10. If Tom enjoyed chess, he would gladly play with me. 11. If we had been in Mexico, we would have gone shopping every afternoon. 12. If you had had a down payment, you could have bought this car. 13. If the weather had been better, the boys would have gone hiking. 14. If my family had lived in the capital, I would have visited the museums every day. 15. If the plane had landed early, we could have gotten downtown by 5 P.M. 16. If she had caught a plane, she might have been in New York by dusk. 17. If I had understood your language, I would have been happy to chat with you. 18. If you had slept longer, you would have had more energy. 19. If the circus had come to town, we would have gone there every day. 20. If Tom had enjoyed chess, he would have gladly played with me.

Exercise 93

1. Would that it were so. 2. The truth be told 3. God bless America! 4. come what may 5. If I were you 6. Far be it for me 7. Heaven forbid! 8. So be it. 9. Suffice it to say 10. If need be.

Exercise 94

1. I could have read the entire novel. I ought to have read the entire novel. I must have read the entire novel. 2. We could have been living in Spain. We might have been living in Spain. We should have been living in Spain. 3. Dad might have repaired the truck. Dad must have repaired the truck. Dad should have repaired the truck. 4. The girls could have memorized the poems. The girls must have memorized the poems. The girls should have memorized the poems. 5. He ought not to have sold the cabin. He must not have sold the cabin. He should not have sold the cabin.

Exercise 95

1. Martin backed up the SUV. Martin has backed up the SUV. Martin will back up the SUV. 2. Jim asked the new girl out. Jim has asked the new girl out. Jim will ask the new girl out. 3. Was Dr. Garcia in today? Has Dr. Garcia been in today? Will Dr. Garcia be in today? 4. They dropped off a gift for the bride. They have dropped off a gift for the bride. They will drop off a gift for the bride. 5. You never gave up on me. You have never given up on me. You will never give up on me. 6. She finally went into her reason for leaving. She finally has gone into her reason for leaving. She finally will go into her reason for leaving. 7. We were heading for Alaska. We have been heading for Alaska. We will be heading for Alaska. 8. John didn't let on about the surprise party. John hasn't let on about the surprise party. John won't let on about the surprise party. 9. Your father put up with a lot. Your father has put up with a lot. Your father will put up with a lot. 10. They set out on a long journey. They have set out on a long journey. They will set out on a long journey. 11. The secretary took down every word. The secretary has taken down every word. The secretary will take down every word. 12. I always threw up on a roller coaster. I have always thrown up on a roller coaster. I will always throw up on a roller coaster. 13. Barbara turned down my offer. Barbara has turned down my offer. Barbara will turn down my offer. 14. Jake slowly warmed up to his boss. Jake has slowly warmed up to his boss. Jake will slowly warm up to his boss. 15. I didn't write off our team this year. I haven't written off our team this year. I won't write off our team this year.

Exercise 96

1. The limousine is being backed up by the chauffeur. 2.The French girl will be asked out by Brian. 3. My statement had been written off by the judge. 4. Their offer has been turned down by the manager. 5. His old friend was written off by him as hopeless.

Exercise 97

1. I should be in by midnight. I should have been in by midnight. I have to be in by midnight. 2. She must try to warm up to him. She can try to warm up to him. She needs to try to warm up to him. 3. You should head for the coast by noon. You ought to head for the coast by noon. You want to head for the coast by noon. 4. Does he need to throw up in the car? Does he have to throw up in the car? Could he have thrown up in the car? 5. She

couldn't always put up with him. She doesn't always like to put up with him. She may not always put up with him. 6. Mary might be out for the day. Mary is supposed to be out for the day. Mary must have been out for the day. 7. Bill shouldn't let on about his new job. Bill mustn't let on about his new job. Bill can't let on about his new job. 8. Where should they drop off their laundry? Where do they have to drop off their laundry? Where should they have dropped off their laundry? 9. The driver can back up here. The driver could have backed up here. The driver wants to back up here. 10. The clerk needs to take down the man's testimony. The clerk ought to have taken down the man's testimony. The clerk could take down the man's testimony.

Exercise 98

1. He backs up the car into the street. He backs the car up into the street. He backs it up into the street. 2. John asks out the pretty girl. John asks the pretty girl out. John asks her out. 3. Mother drops off the children at school. Mother drops the children off at school. Mother drops them off at school. 4. Take down the injured man's statement. Take the injured man's statement down. Take it down. 5. The little boy never turns down candy. The little boy never turns candy down. The little boy never turns it down.

Exercise 99

1. she burns herself 2. I enjoy myself 3. they amuse themselves 4. we perjure ourselves 5. you push yourself 6. it raises itself 7. he calms himself 8. the women fan themselves 9. Bill and I help ourselves 10. you dress yourselves

Exercise 100

1. it is stolen, it is being stolen 2. she is kissed, she is being kissed 3. I am punished, I am being punished 4. the engineer is hired, the engineer is being hired 5. they are broken, they are being broken 6. you are invited, you are being invited 7. the words are spelled, the words are being spelled 8. the men are warned, the men are being warned 9. she is rewarded, she is being rewarded 10. the boy is punished, the boy is being punished 11. the new hotels are built, the new hotels are being built 12. the trees are grown, the trees are being grown 13. no one is suspected, no one is being suspected 14. who is taken, who is being taken 15. something is lost, something is being lost

Exercise 101

1. My wallet was stolen by a pickpocket. My wallet has been stolen by a pickpocket. My wallet had been stolen by a pickpocket. My wallet will be stolen by a pickpocket. 2. Who was accused of the crime? Who has been accused of the crime? Who had been accused of the crime? Who will be accused of the crime? 3. He was being chased by a skunk. He has been chased by a skunk. He had been chased by a skunk. He will be chased by a skunk. 4. The mirror was smashed with a hammer. The mirror has been smashed with a hammer. The mirror had been smashed with a hammer. The mirror will be smashed with a hammer. 5. They were praised by their teacher. They have been praised by their teacher. They had been praised by their teacher. They will be praised by their teacher.

Exercise 102

1. S 2. P 3. P 4. P 5. S

Exercise 103

1. It should not be done. It is not to be done. It must not be done. 2. The floor is supposed to be mopped. The floor ought to have been mopped. The floor has to be mopped.

Exercise 104

1. help, helped 2. see, saw 3. make, made 4. go, went 5. need, needed 6. be, were 7. warn, warned 8. spend, spent 9. eat, ate 10. laugh, laughed 11. have, had 12. drink, drank 13. cut, cut 14. be, were 15. grow, grew

Exercise 105

1. belonged 2. were 3. had 4. could 5. knew 6. had studied 7. worked 8. started 9. were 10. had lived

Exercise 106

1. He could have read the small print. He ought to have read the small print. He must have read the small print. 2. I could have been living in luxury. I might have been living in luxury. I should have been living in luxury. 3. My sister might have fixed the radio. My sister must have fixed the radio. My sister should have fixed the radio. 4. The girl could have memorized Lincoln's Gettysburg Address. The girl must have memorized Lincoln's Gettysburg Address. The girl should have memorized Lincoln's Gettysburg Address. 5. We ought not to have sold our car. We must not have sold our car. We should not have sold our car.

Exercise 107

1. P 2. A 3. A 4. A 5. P 6. A 7. A 8. P 9. A 10. A

Exercise 108

1. Their son should be in by suppertime. Their son should have been in by suppertime. Their son has to be in by suppertime. 2. We must try to warm up to the angry man. We can try to warm up to the angry man. We need to try to warm up to the angry man. 3. He should head for the locker room. He ought to head for the locker room. He wants to head for the locker room.